DATE DUE

OCT 0 4 1990			
DEC 0 4 1990			
APR 1 5 1992			
3-8-99			
GAYLORD			PRINTED IN U..S.A.

THE
RIGHTS
WE HAVE

THE
RIGHTS
WE HAVE

Osmond K. Fraenkel

Second Edition

Revised to include the most important decisions
of the U.S. Supreme Court through 1973

THOMAS Y. CROWELL COMPANY · New York
ESTABLISHED 1834

323.4
F

Acknowledgments

To Alan Reitman of the American Civil Liberties Union for having suggested that I write this book.

To May Freedman at whose home on Deer Isle, Maine, the book was commenced and to her guests for listening to the reading of parts and for their very valuable comments.

To Edward Tripp of the Thomas Y. Crowell Company for his meticulous editing and helpful counsel.

To my secretary, Dorothy Gangel, for her careful deciphering of my scrawl.

To my wife for her constant encouragement and for selecting the title.

Designed by Carole Fern Halpert

Manufactured in the United States of America
L.C. Card 79–158706
ISBN 0–690–00585–7
1 2 3 4 5 6 7 8 9 10
Library of Congress Cataloging in Publication Data
Fraenkel, Osmond Kessler, 1888–
    The rights we have. (Rev. ed.)

    1. Civil rights—United States—Popular works.
I. Title.
KF4750.F69   1973   323.4'0973   74–5428
ISBN 0–690–00585–7

Contents

Contents

Contents

Introduction

Promises of the Declaration of Independence

The Declaration of Independence asserts that all men are "created equal" and entitled to "life, liberty, and the pursuit of happiness." How far have these noble aspirations become the law of the land?

When the Declaration was written equality did not exist for slaves, women, and a large part of the male population. A person's life could be taken on conviction of various crimes. Liberty might be lost on conviction of a host of offenses under safeguards that varied from colony to colony. Nowhere was there legal protection for the pursuit of happiness. But since that time advances have been made in all these areas.

Slavery ended with the Thirteenth Amendment, but the descendants of slaves are still fighting the battle of equality —or, more precisely, the battle against discrimination. Women got the vote more than fifty years ago, but a "Women's Liberation" movement is in full swing. While universal male suffrage was achieved early in the nineteenth century,

real equality in voting has only recently become possible by
reason of the Supreme Court's approval of the "one man, one
vote" principle. And today other minorities—the young, the
homosexual—have become vocal. So the fight for freedom
from discrimination and for true equality goes on.

Capital punishment as imposed by most states is unconstitutional since 1972. The threat of imprisonment on conviction
for crime will naturally continue, but the likelihood that
innocent persons will be convicted has been lessened by the
safeguards of the Bill of Rights and, in the last quarter century, by the Supreme Court's liberal interpretation of these.

The "pursuit of happiness" is still the stepchild of the law.
But the benefits of the Welfare State have provided at least
minimal recognition of this aspiration of the Declaration.
Suggestions such as the provision of a guaranteed income
move in the same direction.

Progress has been made toward giving legal sanction to the
ideals of the Declaration. Just how the individual is really
protected in the rights there declared and others essential to
the working of a democracy is the subject of this book.

The Bill of Rights

The impulse to exact guarantees against absolute power goes
back to the Magna Carta, by which document in 1215 the bar-
ons of England exacted concessions from King John. That
document protected them from punishment except in accordance with the "law of the land," a phrase that was the precur-
sor of the modern "due process." Religious differences with
the English Stuarts led, in the seventeenth century, to various declarations recognizing the rights of subjects against the
crown. Many of the emigrants to North America had some
provisions in their colonial constitutions safeguarding certain

rights. During the Revolution these were incorporated into the constitutions of the newly established states and somewhat enlarged. Perhaps the most notable was Jefferson's Bill for Religious Liberty of Virginia, which said in part that:

> no man shall be compelled to frequent or support any religious worship, place, or ministry whatsoever, nor shall be enforced, restrained, molested, or burthened in his body or goods, nor shall otherwise suffer on account of his religious opinions or belief.

Because various state constitutional provisions already existed, the delegates to the Philadelphia Convention that drafted the Constitution of the United States saw no need to add similar ones. The federal government, they pointed out, was one of limited powers. It was not, they thought, necessary to include safeguards against it. But popular opinion thought otherwise. Several of the states made it clear that they would ratify the Constitution only if a bill of rights were added. So one of the first things done by the newly elected Congress was just that.

This feeling that there must be guarantees against government was, of course, based on the English experience, with which the leaders of the new states were thoroughly familiar. Although the English safeguards were directed against the crown, the colonists well recognized that a majority of even a democratic people might be arbitrary, tyrannical, intolerant of dissent, or impatient with safeguards for those accused of crime. Fresh in the minds of many colonists was their experience with harsh enforcement of British laws aimed particularly at smuggling from the islands of the Caribbean after the French and Indian War.

A considerable number of amendments were proposed, some of which would have restrained the states as well as the federal government. Of the ten that were adopted, not all are of equal importance today. (The text of the Bill of Rights is in Appendix 1.) Each of the guarantees contained in these amendments that has significance for our times will be separately discussed. It is important to note that, until well into the twentieth century, the Supreme Court had ruled that they did not restrict state action, but only action by the federal government.

Collectively these amendments create what, in modern terms, are known as civil liberties. The term "civil rights" has the same meaning, but it is often used especially in speaking of problems of discrimination. Congress enacted a law with this title after the adoption of the post-Civil War amendments in aid of the newly freed slaves. Since that date it has enacted many more, the most recent in 1968. Of those post-Civil War amendments the Thirteenth abolished slavery. The Fourteenth bound the states not to deprive any person of "life, liberty, or property, without due process of law," or deny anyone the "equal protection of the laws." The Fifteenth ensured that the vote should be denied to no one because of "race, color, or previous condition of servitude." (The text of these is in Appendix 2.) Votes for women were, in 1920, guaranteed by the Nineteenth.

These amendments enacted since the Bill of Rights expressly restricted state action. Except for the Thirteenth they did not prohibit action by individuals unless they acted under some state law or custom. It was a long time before the Supreme Court used the "due process" clause of the Fourteenth Amendment to interpret the specific provisions of the Bill of Rights as restrictions on the states as well as on the federal government. This practice began in 1924 when the guarantee of freedom of speech was held to be binding on the states. Soon freedom of assembly and religion were added. But it was not until the last few years of the Warren Court that all provisions of the Bill of Rights (except the requirement of indictment) were held binding on the states. The right to speedy trial was so held in 1967, trial by jury in 1968, and protection against double jeopardy in 1969.

Until these guarantees had become binding on the states an

4

adverse decision by a state court, for instance a decision that a second trial in a particular situation did not constitute double jeopardy (see section 45), could not be brought to the Supreme Court for review.

Many problems have arisen also in connection with claims of infringement of liberties that the Bill of Rights does not appear to guarantee. Sometimes the Court has been able to deal with these by invoking the broad concepts of due process and equal protection. At other times it has had to struggle to find a constitutional basis for a particular decision.

The tremendous growth in the number of civil liberties decisions by the Court in the past quarter century should indicate that the Bill of Rights is as much needed today as it was felt to be needed by the leaders of opinion during the debates on the adoption of the Constitution. But recent polls suggest that a large percentage, perhaps even a majority, of the American people do not now realize this. Many of them are ignorant of the provisions of the Bill of Rights and the reasons that led to their adoption. Others are provoked by the lawless actions of many demonstrators into taking action to preserve "law and order" without regard for individual rights. Too often these persons believe that the safeguards protect only the criminal and the undesirable and that they themselves have no need for them. Their attitude is like that of the person who considers expenditures for traffic cops wasteful, forgetting that in some emergency his own life might be endangered if there were no traffic regulations. So in a revolutionary crisis, if there were no guarantees of individual rights and courts to enforce them no one could be assured of protection against arbitrary arrest and punishment. Recent developments in many parts of the world should alert our "silent majority" to the necessity of maintaining and strengthening all the guarantees of the Bill of Rights. In this book we shall consider to what extent the Congress and the ultimate protector of those guarantees, the Supreme Court of the United States, have done this.

The Supreme Court

The United States Supreme Court is at the head of the federal judiciary. Established by the Constitution (Article III), it was vested with power to decide all cases "arising under this Constitution, the laws of the United States and treaties made. . . ." Except for a few specific grants of original jurisdiction affecting foreign diplomats and controversies between states that are not relevant here, the Constitution gives Congress the right to specify what appellate jurisdiction the Supreme Court shall have—that is, its power to review the decisions of other courts, both state and federal. And, from time to time, Congress has prescribed the ways in which an aggrieved party can get to the Supreme Court. Except in one instance Congress has used this power only to facilitate the business of the Court. But after the Civil War, when it seemed likely that the Court might strike down some of the harsh laws Congress had enacted to "reconstruct" the South, Congress passed a law depriving the Court of jurisdiction to consider any case involving such a law and the Court accepted the limitation imposed on it. In more recent times legislation proposed to curb the Court's activity in certain areas has failed in part, perhaps, because of a belief that the Court would not now be so meek.

Congress has given the Supreme Court complete supervisory power over all the other courts of the United States. But it can review decisions by state courts only if an issue under the United States Constitution, a treaty, or an Act of Congress exists. And even then, the Supreme Court will not consider a state case unless (a) the federal issue was properly raised, (b) the case was taken to the state's highest court, and (c) the federal issue was considered by it. If that court has written an opinion, it will be searched to see how the federal claim was dealt with. But if there was no opinion or one which failed to mention the federal claim, then steps must be taken to get the state court to certify to the Supreme Court that it had considered and denied the federal claim on the basis of which the aggrieved person hopes to get to the Supreme Court (see section 49).

A very dramatic instance of the impact of this requirement occurred in New York many years ago. Section 903 of the New York City Charter required dismissal of employees who refused to testify before any court, legislative committee, or board having authority to conduct an inquiry about matters related to the affairs of the city or their official conduct. Several teachers, when asked in 1952 about Communist affiliations by a congressional committee, pleaded their privilege against self-incrimination and were dismissed. In proceedings challenging these dismissals they all claimed that their right to due process had been denied because the dismissals were automatic and they were given no opportunity to explain. On the way through New York's courts one of the teachers got a different lawyer. In New York's highest court that lawyer argued the constitutional issue; the lawyer for the others relied only on state legal principles. The opinion upholding all the dismissals did not mention the federal issue raised by the one lawyer. When both lawyers then asked the state court to certify to the United States Supreme Court that a federal question had been considered, it did so for the teacher whose lawyer had argued it and refused to do so for the others. In consequence the Supreme Court considered only the case of that one teacher. When after having heard argument it set his dismissal aside, he was reinstated with back pay. The other teachers never were. This was a horrible example of the impact of technicalities that still control the law.

There are some situations in which no appeal is possible under state law. In these cases application for review can be made directly to the Supreme Court. A recent instance of this was a case from Louisville, Kentucky. There a man who had been convicted of disorderly conduct was fined ten dollars. Under state law no fine so small could be appealed. So the case went right to the Supreme Court, which reversed the conviction on the ground that no evidence of disorderly conduct had been produced.

Congress has provided two methods for review of a state decision. The first is by appeal "as of right" where the issue is whether a state law or municipal ordinance is valid under the United States Constitution. The second is by writ of certiorari at the discretion of the Supreme Court. Certiorari is the only method by which one can go to the Supreme Court to review a conviction in a federal court. Very few applications for certiorari are granted, although the vote of four justices is sufficient to grant one. Failure to grant such an application is not a decision on the merits of the case. Several opinions have been written explaining the rationale of the Court. Often such applications are denied because the Court does not think the issue is "ripe" for adjudication—which is a way of saying that the Court hopes the issue will not recur to plague it. That happened in the Jehovah's Witnesses flag salute cases (see section 3a) and in a number of challenges to the right of the House Committee on Un-American Activities to question witnesses, which we shall refer to later (see section 16a). Sometimes certiorari is refused because the federal issue was not clearly enough presented. If certiorari is granted the case will ordinarily be argued before the Court. But in recent years the Court has frequently granted the application and at the same time reversed the conviction without hearing argument.

Even though an appeal can be taken "as of right," that does not mean there will be argument. The Court requires the lawyer to file a "jurisdictional statement." This must show the basis for going to the Court, show that the federal issue was properly presented in the state court, and demonstrate that it has substance. If one or another of these requirements has not been met the Court will dismiss the appeal for want of a "substantial federal question" or because that question had not been properly raised. The former comment is made if the Court thinks the point raised has already been decided or is frivolous. The latter was made in the case of the New York teachers.

It is almost unprecedented for the Court to announce its decision at once. The practice of the Court is to hold conferences each week. After a preliminary vote the Chief assigns the writing of the majority opinion, which is then circulated among the justices. It may turn out that reflection has changed a vote or two so that what started out as a majority opinion becomes a dissent. Any justice can write a dissent, or even a concurring opinion. In one set of three related cases there were fourteen opinions. It sometimes happens that only four of the justices will agree with the majority opinion on the grounds set forth in it, so that no binding precedent is established by the decision. There are also cases in which, because of the absence or disqualification of one of the justices, the Court is evenly divided. In such a case the decision of the lower court stands, but no precedent has been made. The issue, therefore, remains open for someone else to bring up in another case, and ordinarily no opinion is written. When that happens the Court sometimes sets the case down for reargument when the ninth justice becomes available.

Ordinarily all federal cases are reviewed only by the discretionary method of certiorari. But Congress has set up a special procedure for handling cases in which a complainant seeks to enjoin enforcement of a law on the ground that it is unconstitutional. (This procedure is not, however, applicable to an attack on a local ordinance.) The issue of constitutionality cannot be decided by a single judge. It can be decided only by a so-called statutory court called to consider the particular case. This consists of three judges, two from the District Court and one from the Court of Appeals. From their decision there is a direct appeal "as of right" to the United States Supreme Court. But there can be all kinds of complications. If the District Court judge before whom the case is started believes that the constitutional issue raised is frivolous, he will dismiss the case without calling for the three-judge court.

Then an appeal can be taken only to the Court of Appeals. That court may disagree and, instead of passing on the constitutional issue itself, send the case back to the District Court to have a three-judge court convened. The process can be time-consuming, costly, and frustrating. This actually happened in a case we shall discuss (see section 12e) of a bachelor residing with his parents who wanted to vote in a school district election. It took forty months before the case was finally decided in his favor by the Supreme Court. Had it not been for the sponsorship of the New York Civil Liberties Union, it is doubtful whether the plaintiff would have been able to support so much litigation. But no direct appeal can be taken to the Supreme Court if the three-judge court has issued a declaratory judgment declaring a law unconstitutional but has declined to enjoin its enforcement.

The usefulness of this statutory court procedure was considerably restricted by six decisions rendered in February 1971 in which seventeen opinions were written. The general rule was laid down that a federal court should not interfere with state prosecutions even if it concluded that the state law was unconstitutional or was being unconstitutionally applied unless "exceptional circumstances" could be shown. (For a fuller discussion of these cases see section 49.)

It is evident, therefore, that it is difficult to get to the United States Supreme Court. It takes much time and patience as well as, in most cases, a considerable amount of money. We shall now consider the situation of the justices themselves and the way the business of the Court is conducted.

According to the Constitution (Art. III, Sec. 1) all federal judges hold office "during good behavior." However, like any other civil officer, a justice of the Supreme Court may be removed by impeachment for "treason, bribery, or other high crimes and misdemeanors" (Art. II, Sec. 4). These latter, however, are not defined. The power to initiate an impeachment is vested in the House of Representatives (Art. I, Sec. 2, cl. 5); the power to try in the Senate (Art. I, Sec. 3, cl. 6).

There has been only one impeachment proceeding against a justice of the Supreme Court, that of Samuel Chase in 1805. It was brought on the theory, voiced by Senator Giles of Virginia, that a judge could be removed because of dislike of his opinions. Justice Chase was acquitted. The cases of two lower federal court judges who were impeached leave in some doubt whether the "high crimes and misdemeanors" are limited to indictable offenses, as Chase's counsel had argued. The question of impeachment has been raised recently in connection with former Chief Justice Earl Warren and with Justice William O. Douglas. No formal steps were ever taken against Earl Warren and no one ever seriously questioned his integrity. The outcry against him was wholly political, motivated by conservative dislike for some of his opinions. Douglas, on the other hand, was investigated by a committee of the House of Representatives in 1970 because of some of his outside financial involvements and provocative writings. But nothing came of this.

In the early years the Court sat in a small room in the Capitol. After that was enlarged the Court used what had been until then the Senate Chamber. But in 1935 the Court moved into its present quarters, a marble palace with many corridors and a few fountains. The courtroom has poor acoustics. Often it is impossible for the spectators to hear questions put by the justices. That varies, of course, with the individual justice's voice and power of projection. There is a space in front reserved for lawyers admitted to practice before the Court.

Anyone can come in to the larger area behind but often there are waiting lines. That is particularly the case when the Court is sitting during school vacation time, as then busloads of people come to Washington from all over the country and many visit the Court. Any lawyer who is arguing a case can arrange with the marshal to have a friend or relative he wants to be able to hear him placed in a special section at the right side of the chamber. But it is well to arrange this in advance as the section is small. On decision days the room is likely to be crowded, especially if it has become known that a decision in an important case is coming down. On the occasion of the gold clause case in 1935, which upheld President Franklin D. Roosevelt's devaluation of the dollar, there was barely standing room.

The Court until 1961 used to meet at noon, sit for two hours, recess for half an hour, resume at two-thirty and sit until four-thirty. Now it meets at ten and since March 30, 1970, recesses for an hour and then sits for two more hours. Formerly the Court sat five days a week, with conferences on Saturdays. Now it sits for only four days, with conferences on Fridays. Of course, it does not sit all the time. Generally the sessions last two weeks, including, always, a third Monday. The recesses vary considerably.

The associate justices are seated in order of seniority, first on the right side of the Chief, then on his left and so on down. The most recent appointee, therefore, sits on the extreme right of the bench as seen by the persons in the chamber.

Until late in 1970 the first business every day was the admission of attorneys. Each applicant appeared with a sponsor who was addressed by name by the Chief Justice. The applicants were presented in the order of the importance of their sponsors. The Attorney General had precedence; Senators came before Congressmen. There seemed to be no particular order of preference among ordinary lawyers. The same sponsor might appear for several applicants. Indeed, there were occasions when a host of applicants from a particular area were proposed by one sponsor.

There was a formula for the presentation: "I have examined the papers on file and *believe* that the applicant has the necessary qualifications." When the writer proposed his daughter, he changed the formula to say "I know" that she has those qualifications.

After the applicants had all been presented they were sworn in and required to go to the Clerk's office to sign the rolls and pay the fee. Now they simply file their papers, pay the $25 fee, and get an engraved certificate.

Decisions used to be announced by the Court only on Mondays except in an unusual situation. Since 1965 that is no longer the case. While the orders of the Court are still announced on Mondays, opinions are announced on other days. The Chief will call on the justices in reverse order of seniority to announce the decisions in the cases in which they have written the majority opinion. The announcement can be brief or lengthy, as the justice decides. Any other justice who has written a concurring or dissenting opinion usually adds his bit. Dissenters are often highly critical of the majority, sometimes bitter and emotional. They sometimes say things not reflected in their written opinions. After Chief Justice Hughes announced the decision in 1935 upholding President Franklin D. Roosevelt's devaluation of the dollar, Justice McReynolds thundered, "The Constitution is dead."

Reporters in the courtroom send accounts of decisions down tubes to assistants waiting below to telephone them to their papers. Important decisions are carried to brokerage offices on news tickers, especially if they affect financial matters. Many years ago a news item appeared based on a reporter's guess from the early recital of the decision that affected the price of the stock of the corporation involved in the case which turned out to have been a wrong guess.

The bulk of the Court's decisions are without opinion and are not announced from the bench. The Chief Justice simply says that the list of orders is on file with the Clerk.

Following the announcements come the arguments. Often, however, on the Monday preceding a recess the Court hears no arguments.

Since the Constitution did not fix the number of justices, Congress has, on a number of occasions, done so. The number has been nine for nearly a century. It will be recalled that in

1937 President Franklin D. Roosevelt proposed an increase to fifteen. He gave as his reason the age of some of the incumbents and suggested that new blood would enable the Court to handle its business more efficiently. Actually, of course, FDR was motivated by a desire to circumvent the many decisions of the Court which had struck down some of his pet New Deal measures. The proposal aroused so much opposition that it died in the Congress. But the airing of the problem accomplished the President's objective. Justice Roberts changed his position in a vital minimum wage case, some of the hard core conservatives took advantage of a new retirement measure which passed, and FDR was at last, after more than four years in office, able to put new men on the Court.

Nowhere in the Constitution is the Supreme Court given the power to declare laws of Congress unconstitutional. But almost at the beginning of its existence the Court exercised that power under the leadership of John Marshall. Many writers have challenged the Court's right to take such action, but the Court has never abandoned its position. Indeed, it is difficult to see how any meaning could be attached to a Bill of Rights unless the Court could void any law which violated it. During the debates which preceded the ratification of the Constitution, this view was expressed with regard to those provisions in the original Constitution which restricted both the federal and state governments. A series of papers were published under assumed names which came to be known as the Federalist Papers and which discussed all the aspects of the proposed Constitution. One of these (No. 78, now known to have been written by Alexander Hamilton) said:

> Limitations of this kind can be preserved in practice no other way than through the medium of the courts of justice; whose duty it must be to declare all acts contrary to the manifest tenor of the Constitution void. Without this, all the reservations of particular rights or privileges would amount to nothing.

The way in which the Court has exercised its power has been continuously criticized, and still is. At present most of the criticism is directed at what is called the "activist" position of the Court in the field of civil liberties, which reached its highest point under the leadership of Earl Warren. Actually it began under Charles Evans Hughes after the injection of the new blood of FDR's appointments, and continued under Harlan F. Stone. It was slowed up under Fred Vinson, then burst into full bloom under Warren.

Before the present wave of pro-civil liberties decisions, Oliver Wendell Holmes and Louis D. Brandeis were in frequent dissent; they were joined from time to time by Stone. After Holmes's retirement, his place on the liberal minority was taken by Benjamin N. Cardozo. Many of these dissents were later accepted as doctrine by the Court. For it must be remembered that the Court has never hesitated to overrule old decisions. That practice has led to the belief that the Court acts politically or, as Finley Peter Dunne had his character Mr. Dooley say early in the century, that it follows the election returns. To some extent this appears to be the case. But it must be borne in mind that the Court is interpreting a Constitution written in broad terms which are not subject to precise, mechanical definition. It is inevitable, therefore, that as the climate of opinion constantly changes justices will be appointed who hold the new views.

For example, in the late nineteenth century the Court found in the clause of the Fourteenth Amendment, which guarantees against deprivation of "life, liberty, or property, without due process of law," a "liberty of contract," which justified it in striking down a host of state and federal laws that sought to regulate industry. An instance of this arose early in the present century in connection with "Yellow Dog Contracts." These were agreements exacted by employers that their employees would not join labor unions. When Congress and some states passed laws banning such contracts the

Supreme Court struck them down on the theory that they violated the employees' freedom of contract, ignoring the fact that the economic power of the employer was depriving the employee of his freedom and that the new laws were designed to correct this imbalance. That was in a period of industrial expansion following the Civil War. As the evils attendant upon that expansion became better known a revulsion set in, although it took FDR's Court-packing plan to set it off.

Similarly, after the harsh repression of dissent during and after World War I, a new interest in civil liberties developed. Its impact on the law forms the subject of this book. The first evidences of this interest were in the Court's dissenting opinions already mentioned, from some of which we shall later quote. A number of notable decisions were handed down under Hughes by the old Court: Scottsboro, DeJonge, Herndon. But the impetus developed as the new men came to the Court.

The first and most notable of these was Hugo L. Black, who died at eighty-five. He had been a vigorous senator. Serious opposition to him developed when it was learned that he had, in his youth, been a member of the Ku Klux Klan. His activities on the Court soon made it evident that he had not been infected by that affiliation. He had become the most vocal supporter of freedom of expression and opponent of discrimination. Though criticized as an "activist," he maintained that he was only a strict constructionist. And some of his more recent opinions bear this out.

Of FDR's other appointees, only William O. Douglas is still on the Court. He had been a teacher of law and head of the Securities and Exchange Commission. In the vast majority of cases he and Black have been on the same side—often, in the beginning, in dissent. But in recent years they have often disagreed. Douglas has been much in the public eye on account of various marital changes, much mountain climbing, and many books.

16

Perhaps the most controversial and, in some ways, the most influential of FDR's other appointees was Felix Frankfurter. He had for years been a professor at the Harvard Law School. He had sent many brilliant young men to Washington to serve as law clerks to the justices. He had aroused controversy by an article, later expanded into a book, protesting the unfairness of the Sacco-Vanzetti trial. He had become an adviser to FDR at the time of the New Deal. No one ever questioned his great ability, but as a justice he disappointed many. That was due to his adherence to the view, so approved by all liberals during the "liberty of contract" phase of the Court, that laws should be upheld if they served a reasonable legislative purpose. That view, when applied to the field of civil liberties, often led him to take positions that offended ardent libertarians.

Perhaps the most famous instance was the case involving the right of local school authorities to discipline Jehovah's Witnesses because their children refused to take part in flag salute ceremonies. Frankfurter wrote the opinion which upheld the authorities against the claim of the Witnesses that the religious freedom of the children was being impaired. At the time Justice Stone was the only dissenter. And when a few years later the Court reversed itself, Frankfurter maintained his position in dissent:

We are told that a flag salute is a doubtful substitute for adequate understanding of our institutions. The states that require such a school exercise do not have to justify it as the only means for promoting good citizenship in children, but merely as one of diverse means for accomplishing a worthy end. We may deem it a foolish measure, but the point is that this Court is not the organ of government to resolve doubts as to whether it will fulfill its purpose. Only if there be no doubt that any reasonable mind could entertain can we deny to the states the right to resolve doubts their way and not ours.

That which to the majority may seem essential for the welfare of the state may offend the consciences of a minority. But, so long as no inroads are made upon the actual exercise of religion by the minority, to deny the political power of the majority to enact laws concerned with civil matters, simply because they may offend the consciences of a minority, really means that the consciences of a minority are more sacred and more enshrined in the Constitution than the consciences of a majority.

We are told that symbolism is a dramatic but primitive way of communicating ideas. Symbolism is inescapable. Even the most sophisticated live by symbols. But it is not for this Court to make psychological judgments as to the effectiveness of a particular symbol in inculcating concededly indispensable feelings, particularly if the state happens to see fit to utilize the symbol that represents our heritage and our hopes [319 U.S. 624, 1943].

Of the justices who sat in 1973 none are left whom Truman had appointed. Brennan and Stewart were appointed by Eisenhower (as Warren had been); White by Kennedy; Marshall by Johnson; and Burger, Blackmun, Powell, and Rehnquist by Nixon. (Appendix 3 shows the tenures of justices between 1945 and 1973.)

John M. Harlan, who had been appointed by President Eisenhower, retired in the fall of 1971 and died a few months later. He was the grandson and namesake of that Harlan who, at the turn of the century, dissented from many decisions now repudiated. The young Harlan had been a member of one of New York's great law firms, at one time headed by Elihu Root.

William J. Brennan, Jr., the only Catholic on the Court, had been a judge in New Jersey. He has surprised many by his liberal attitude, generally siding with Black and Douglas. Byron R. White had been a friend of Kennedy's, Potter Stewart a federal judge.

Thurgood Marshall had for years been chief counsel for the NAACP, sat on the Court of Appeals for the Second Circuit, and then became Solicitor General. His devotion to civil liberties is self-evident. The other Kennedy and Johnson appointees, Arthur Goldberg and Abe Fortas, resigned, the first to become our representative at the United Nations, later defeated in the race for governor of New York. The second was defeated for the Chief Justiceship, and later resigned because of past financial affiliations with one Wolfson.

Chief Justice Burger served for years on the Court of Appeals for the District of Columbia Circuit; Harry A. Blackmun sat on the Court of Appeals for the Eighth Circuit. Lewis F. Powell had been a president of the American Bar Association; William H. Rehnquist an Assistant Attorney General under Mr. Mitchell. Neither had any prior judicial experience; both were regarded as conservatives at the time of their appointment. Undoubtedly President Nixon believes they will reflect his own views.

At the 1972 Term President Nixon's appointees were part of a 5-4 majority in eighteen cases, sixteen with the concurrence of Justice White, two with Justice Stewart. Although none of those decisions actually overruled any of the Warren Court's rulings, all had a limiting effect on the area of civil liberties. The impact of the two new justices is bound to be serious and may even result in some express repudiation of earlier liberal doctrine.

It has happened that Presidents have been disappointed by the positions taken by their appointees. Theodore Roosevelt appointed Oliver Wendell Holmes expecting that he would take the government's view of antitrust cases and found out otherwise in the Northern Securities case. Surely Eisenhower did not expect Earl Warren to become the liberal Chief that he did.

The Congress

As Justice Frankfurter was fond of reminding us, the Supreme Court is not the only organ of government responsible for the preservation of liberty. Clearly the elected representatives of the people assembled in the Congress have as great a responsibility. Because they are elected, it was thought that they might be more sensitive to the needs of the people than the appointed justices of the Supreme Court. One trouble with that point of view, however, is that Congress, in any particular session, represents a passing majority. The Bill of Rights was expressly designed to curb the power of just such a majority.

Nevertheless, Congress can have an important impact on our liberties, both by restricting them and by enlarging them. It has done so and continues both to enlarge and to restrict, though in different areas of its powers. These are expressly limited in the Constitution, so that Congress does not have the power the states have to make acts criminal. The states and their subdivisions have the right, subject ultimately to review by the courts, to make criminal any offense committed within their borders, such as murder, rape, theft, arson, the sale (and sometimes the mere possession) of obscene material or narcotics, and a whole host of minor offenses such as trespass, rioting, disorderly conduct, reckless driving.

The main areas of congressional power are interstate and foreign commerce, the mails, national safety, and the armed forces.

Familiar criminal laws resting on the commerce clause are the Lindbergh kidnapping law, with its death penalty; the Mann Act, which punishes transportation of a woman across state lines for an immoral purpose; and the Securities and Exchange Commission laws, which regulate transactions in securities when, for example, an interstate telephone call is made. Possession of narcotics can be a federal offense because Congress can forbid their importation. The law under which the Chicago Seven were convicted also comes within the interstate commerce category: travel across state lines with intent to cause a riot. The constitutionality of this law was upheld on appeal in that case. Use of the mails to defraud or to transport obscene material makes punishable in a federal court an act that would otherwise be only a state offense. Congress also has full and exclusive power over offenses committed against the armed forces, the recruitment services, or the draft. All the problems of improper classification or induction of registrants come to the federal courts (see section 6a). As a matter of fact, Congress could make federal jurisdiction exclusive also in other areas of its own power and so debar state courts from dealing with such subjects at all.

Congress has the same power over crimes committed in the District of Columbia as any state has with respect to its own area. The same is true of the few territories that still exist, such as Samoa. Federal land within a state, as for example an army base or a national park, may or may not be under the control of federal law, depending on the arrangements that were made at the time the land was ceded to the federal government.

The very first congressional assault on freedom was the enactment in 1798 of the Alien and Sedition Laws, motivated in part by fear of the French Revolution and by President Adams' reaction to a critical press. Many newspaper editors went to jail, but were later released by Jefferson when he became president in 1801. The general opinion among jurists is that these laws were unconstitutional, but no case under them reached the Supreme Court.

Indeed, no test of congressional power in the area of expression of opinion reached the Supreme Court until after World War I. Then the Court upheld the prosecution of various leaders of the Socialist party, including its candidate for the presidency, Eugene V. Debs, for their speeches opposing our participation in that war on the ground that those speeches violated the Espionage Act of 1917.

The "cold war" against Soviet Russia that began after World War II in 1945 and the McCarthy hysteria of the fifties produced more restrictive legislation. President Truman vetoed the McCarran Act of 1950 on the ground that it was patently unconstitutional, but Congress passed it over his veto. That law created the Subversive Activities Control Board, aimed primarily at the Communist party and its "action" and "front" organizations. While the Supreme Court has not declared the law unconstitutional, it has restricted its operation (see section 14b). The law's most dangerous provision, for "Emergency Detention of Suspected Security Risks," has fortunately never been put in operation.

More recently, in 1970, Congress passed crime bills for the District of Columbia and in connection with organized crime that contain many provisions interfering with the liberty of persons. They will no doubt be challenged as these provisions are, from time to time, put in effect.

On the other hand, Congress has passed many laws that have enlarged freedom. After the Civil War (in 1866, 1870, 1871, and 1875) it enacted a number of civil rights acts in aid of the newly freed Negroes. Many of their provisions were voided or emasculated by Supreme Court decisions, but a number are still in effect and are being enforced. In recent times new civil rights acts have been passed (in 1957, 1960, 1964, and 1968), the next to the last of which prohibited discrimination in employment on the ground of sex as well as race, color, etc. (see section 10a). In 1970 Congress passed a law to give eighteen-year-old persons the right to vote. The Supreme Court held this to be valid only for national elections. It was a 5 to 4 decision (see section 12a).

Early in 1971 Congress sent to the states an amendment ensuring voting rights to persons 18 years and older. Ratified in June, it became the Twenty-Sixth Amendment.

Congress has also in modern times helped labor. In 1932 it passed the Norris-LaGuardia Act, which severely limits the power of federal courts to issue injunctions in labor disputes. In 1926 came the Railway Labor Act and in 1935 the Wagner Act. The latter, for the first time, gave a union the right to bargain exclusively when it represented a majority of the workers.

From time to time Congress has recommended to the states various constitutional amendments which have enlarged rights. The three post-Civil War amendments, the Thirteenth, Fourteenth, and Fifteenth, are the most important. They were followed by the Seventeenth (1913), which provided for the popular election of Senators, and the Nineteenth (1920), which gave the vote to women. The Twenty-third gave the District of Columbia votes in the Electoral College (1961). The Twenty-fourth barred the use of the poll tax as qualification for voting for any federal office (1964). In 1972 Congress sent to the states an "Equal Rights" amendment to forbid discrimination on the basis of sex. It is likely to be ratified quickly and to become the Twenty-seventh Amendment.

A Note of Warning

In these pages you will be told that you have certain constitutionally guaranteed rights of protection against governmental interference. In almost all instances the statements that will be made rest on the authority of decisions by the United States Supreme Court. Such decisions are supposed to control all governmental agencies, since the Supreme Court has the last word on what the United States Constitution means.

But unfortunately the facts of life are otherwise. In many areas local law enforcement agencies and sometimes even local judges act as though the Supreme Court had never laid down any rule governing a particular situation. This fact is due mostly to ignorance, frequently to prejudice, sometimes to willfulness. Too often police and prosecuting officials proceed on the theory that the persons caught in their nets have neither the knowledge nor the means to fight illegal practices. And that is all too true. It must be kept in mind that a

Supreme Court decision, except when it declares a law to be unconstitutional, is not self-executing. The same observations apply to the discipline of students.

Every citizen, therefore, has an obligation to try to elect to office local officials committed to the protection of the liberty of individuals, who can be counted on to appoint police chiefs and school officials who will see to it that the men under their command will follow the law as laid down by the courts. It is still true, as Wendell Phillips said more than a century ago, that "eternal vigilance is the price of liberty."

Rights to
Personal Freedom

Among rights that can be described as personal are those that
relate to one's mind, one's home, and one's body. Among the
first are the great First Amendment rights: freedom of expression, freedom of religion, and freedom of assembly. The
second category is embodied in the Fourth Amendment. The
third is somewhat harder to classify. It includes, for women,
the right to have an abortion, and, for men, the whole military complex. Both sexes are protected against slavery, both
have the right to travel. To some extent these overlap; to
some extent also constitutional guarantees such as the right
to due process come into play.

1. The Right to Express Oneself

Of all the constitutional guarantees the right to speak one's
mind is the most important. Without it there can be no liberty. This right is enshrined in the First Amendment: "Con-

gress shall make no law . . . abridging the freedom of speech,
or of the press. . . ."

The Supreme Court has both enlarged and restricted this
guarantee. It has enlarged it by applying it to all government
authority—federal, state, or local; executive, legislative, or
judicial. It has restricted it by upholding certain limitations
on expression and by excluding from its scope the obscene
and, to some extent, the defamatory.

Certain basic philosophical considerations have been advanced to justify particular interpretations of the First
Amendment. First and foremost is the "absolutist" view that
the Constitution means just what it says. This is the view of
Justice Hugo L. Black, a "strict constructionist," and it is
often shared by his colleague Justice William O. Douglas.
This view is in fact so absolutist that these justices completely reject the Court's conclusion that obscenity can be
banned (see section 1c). To them the words of the First
Amendment cannot be construed to mean anything less than
that *no law can be passed that restricts free expression.*

Just after World War I the "clear and present danger" test
was formulated by Justice Oliver Wendell Holmes in a case
which upheld the conviction under the Espionage Act of 1917
of the secretary of the Socialist party for obstructing recruiting during the war. He said (*Schenck* v. *United States,* 249
U.S. 47, 1919):

The most stringent protection of free speech would not protect
a man in falsely shouting fire in a theatre and causing a panic.
It does not even protect a man from an injunction against utter-
ing words that may have all the effect of force. . . . The question in every case is whether the words used are used in such circumstances and are of such a nature as to create a clear and
present danger that they will bring about the substantive evils
that Congress has a right to prevent. It is a question of proxim-
ity and degree. When a nation is at war many things that might
be said in time of peace are such a hindrance to its effort that
their utterance will not be endured so long as men fight and
that no Court could regard them as protected by any constitutional right.

In other words, the Court then ruled that speech can be punished when the danger that it will result in illegal action is serious and imminent. Somewhat later Holmes's colleague, Justice Louis D. Brandeis, gave this formula eloquent expression (*Whitney* v. *California*, 274 U.S. 357, 1927):

> Those who won our independence by revolution were not cowards. They did not fear political change. They did not exalt order at the cost of liberty. To courageous, self-reliant men, with confidence in the power of free and fearless reasoning applied through the processes of popular government, no danger flowing from speech can be deemed clear and present, unless the incidence of the evil apprehended is so imminent that it may befall before there is opportunity for full discussion. If there be time to expose through discussion the falsehood and fallacies, to avert the evil by the processes of education, the remedy to be applied is more speech, not enforced silence.

Another criterion for testing restriction on expression is the "balancing" principle, whose most vocal advocate was Justice Felix Frankfurter. According to this principle, speech can be punished if the social good to be accomplished by its suppression is greater than the individual's need to express himself. The fallacy of that test, however, seems to be that it weighted the scales against the individual by ignoring the basic truth that freedom of expression is guaranteed not for the benefit of individual self-expression but to insure that the community has the benefit of every conceivable point of view; that truth can be tested in the marketplace.

This point of view was recognized by a federal three-judge court in 1971 when it ruled unconstitutional a provision of the McCarran Act which barred from entry into the United States persons advocating the forcible overthrow of government. The decision was rendered in a case brought by the excluded person, Dr. Mandel, a Belgian Marxist, and professors in several American universities which had invited him to lecture. Judge Dooling stressed that the First Amendment guaranteed "to the people as sovereign" their right to "an open and wide-ranging debate, publication and assembly, to review the government they have created, the adequacy of its functioning, and the presence or absence of a need to alter or displace it."

The Supreme Court has struck down some state laws because they affected freedom of expression by reason of "overbreadth" and did not specifically aim at any evil the state had a right to control. The doctrine was applied in 1963 when the Court, in a suit brought by the NAACP, held unconstitutional a Virginia law that subjected to discipline any lawyer who was recommended to a litigant by an association that was not financially interested in the case. The Court said that the activities of the NAACP in sponsoring litigation to vindicate the civil rights of Negroes were protected by the First Amendment and were seriously restricted by the Virginia statute. Justices Clark, Harlan, and Stewart dissented.

Both the states and the federal government have enacted laws creating offenses which sometimes infringe on liberty of expression. Since the states have a much wider jurisdiction than the federal government, most of the cases that have reached the United States Supreme Court started in one of the states. For the federal government can exercise only such powers as are specifically mentioned in the Constitution, such as those over interstate and foreign commerce, over the mails, and over the armed forces.

Rights can also be restricted in other situations, as when privileges are affected. The right to get and keep a job and the rights of teachers and students have often been affected by their expressions of opinion. These problems exist in regard to both public service and private employment and institutions.

Generally a person can be dismissed from private employment without any redress. But a public employee may be protected by laws, usually called civil service laws, which give him some kind of tenure and provide for procedures whereby he can meet charges and review a disciplinary measure or dismissal in the courts. A private employee has fewer rights. Even if he has a contract for a fixed term he cannot compel his employer to keep him; he can only get the compensation he would have been entitled to under the contract. However, under various state and federal laws a person dismissed for union activity can get reinstatement. There are also laws forbidding discrimination in hiring by reason of race or sex. But the basic question here is to what extent an employee is protected against discipline or dismissal for the exercise of his constitutional right of expression. (For the consequences of an employee's invoking his privilege against self-incrimination see section 37. For questions of free speech involving labor relations see section 15a.)

1a. *Sedition*

You can express hostility to government, even discuss the desirability of overthrowing it by force.

You cannot urge others to overthrow the government by force.

The term "sedition" is not one that can be defined with any precision. It is often used as an epithet for the words or acts of those who are dissatisfied with things as they are. In eighteenth-century Scotland, the idea of universal suffrage was considered so revolutionary that its advocates were called seditious by some judges. Here we shall deal with laws passed by some states and the federal government which are aimed primarily at those who advocate forcible overthrow of the government.

Governments, like most individuals, want to continue to exist. Thus laws are passed to punish attempts at revolution. Even our own government, despite its violent birth, has such laws. Insofar as they deal with acts, they need not concern us in this section. But alarm over the Russian Revolution of 1917 led a number of states to pass "criminal syndicalism" laws to punish the "advocacy" of the violent overthrow of government. And in 1940 the federal government followed suit with what has become known as the Smith Act.

The Supreme Court, in the twenties, upheld the right of the states to pass laws of this kind, but it did not always approve the way they were applied. Thus, when Oregon punished a member of the Communist party for speaking at a meeting sponsored by that party without any proof that he advocated anything unlawful, the Supreme Court reversed his conviction. Chief Justice Hughes said (*DeJonge* v. *Oregon*, 299 U.S. 353, 1937):

> The greater the importance of safeguarding the community from incitements to the overthrow of our institutions by force and violence, the more imperative is the need to preserve inviolate the constitutional rights of free speech, free press and free assembly in order to maintain the opportunity for free political discussion, to the end that government may be responsive to the will of the people and that changes, if desired, may be obtained by peaceful means. Therein lies the security of the Republic, the very foundation of constitutional government.
>
> It follows from these considerations that, consistently with the Federal Constitution, peaceful assembly for lawful discussion cannot be made a crime. The holding of meetings for peaceable political action cannot be proscribed. Those who assist in the conduct of such meetings cannot be branded as criminals on that score. The question, if the rights of free speech and peaceable assembly are to be preserved, is not as to the auspices under which the meeting is held but as to its purpose; not as to the relations of the speakers, but whether their utterances transcend the bounds of the freedom of speech which the Constitution protects.

Years later the Court upheld the conviction under the Smith Act of the top leaders of the Communist party for con-

spiracy to advocate the overthrow of the government by
force. The Court felt that there was basis for finding sufficient danger that their words might result in illegal action
because of the situation of the American Communist party in
relation to the world Communist movement. In a later case,
however, the Court made it clear that no individual could be
convicted under that law unless he did more than discuss revolution. There must be evidence that he incited (that is,
urged) people to rebel. Moreover, the Court held that no one
could be convicted for mere membership in an organization
that advocated the violent overthrow of the government (as,
according to many decisions, the Communist party did) without proof of his active participation in the illegal advocacy itself.

In 1965 the Court struck down a Louisiana law because it
provided that the findings of the Attorney General of the
United States and various congressional and legislative committees that certain organizations were "subversive" were
presumptive evidence of their character. Justice Brennan
stressed the importance of freedom of expression as "of transcendent value to all society, and not merely to those exercising their rights [380 U.S. 479]."

The Court held in 1969 that an Ohio law similar to the
Smith Act was void because it did not require incitement as
an element of the crime.

It does not seem likely that the ordinary individual will fall
afoul of any of these laws. Yet they can be used to harass people espousing causes that are unpopular in their areas. That
happened to Jehovah's Witnesses in Mississippi during World
War II. The Witnesses were charged with distributing
printed matter which tended "to create an attitude of stub-
born refusal to salute, honor and respect the flag and government of the United States." They were sentenced in 1942 to a
term of ten years or until the end of the war, whichever occurred sooner. The evidence consisted of statements and

printed matter expressing the opinions of the Witnesses critical of government in general and of President Franklin D.
Roosevelt in particular. The Supreme Court set the convictions aside on the ground that no unlawful action had been
advocated. Later Kentucky used a similar law as a net with
which to catch some advocates of school integration. In both
instances state convictions had to be taken to the Supreme
Court before the charges were held unfounded. So long as
such laws remain on the books, they will inevitably tend to
discourage dissent even though such dissent is entirely lawful.

1b. *Disorderly Conduct*

You can say annoying things to an audience.
*You cannot say something offensive to the person directly
addressed.*

Disorderly conduct is an all-embracing term that includes
so many things it all but defies definition. Generally it includes almost anything that might lead to a breach of the
peace. Laws against disorderly conduct can, therefore, easily
be used to restrict free expression. It is the crime with which
the ordinary citizen is most likely to be charged. Here we consider only those aspects of the subject which deal with speech.
Some years ago the Supreme Court suggested that the
touchstone was the use of what it called fighting words. Thus
it overturned the conviction of a person who played records
that strongly criticized the Catholic Church because the circumstances did not indicate the probability of forcible retalia-
tion, but upheld that of a man who called a policeman a rack-
eteer to his face because of the likelihood of forcible response.
On somewhat the same theory the Court, over strong dissent,
upheld the conviction of a street speaker who urged direct action by Negroes and refused to stop speaking when ordered to

do so by a policeman who feared that listeners in the crowd might resort to violence against the speaker. On the other hand, it held that a lower court had been wrong to convict a person for speaking in a hall merely because there was an outburst of resentment outside. In 1971 the Court held that a person who, in a court corridor, wore a jacket on the back of which was written a four-letter word condemning the draft could not be convicted of "offensive conduct."

1c. *Obscenity*

You can freely discuss matters relating to sex and you can privately possess pornography.

You cannot participate in distributing "hard core pornography," but it is hard to determine what materials fall under this definition.

Obscene matter is said to be outside the protection of the First Amendment altogether.

The extent to which it is safe to talk about, write on, or portray sexual matter has tremendously changed in the recent past. There is, of course, a line beyond which it is not safe. But no one has been able to come up with a satisfactory definition of obscenity.

The Supreme Court attempted to do so in the *Roth* case. Two cases were considered together. In one, Roth was convicted under a federal law which forbids use of the mails to distribute obscene matter; in the other, one Alberts was convicted in California for selling obscene material. The Supreme Court was urged in briefs filed by, as friends of the Court, Morris L. Ernst, The Authors League of America, the American Civil Liberties Union, and some publishers to hold that prosecutions for obscenity violated the First Amendment. While the Court refused to do this and upheld both convictions, it did limit the scope of such prosecutions. Justice Brennan said (354 U.S. 476, 1957):

All ideas having even the slightest redeeming social significance—unorthodox ideas, controversial ideas, even ideas hateful to the prevailing climate of opinion—have the full protection of the guaranties, unless excludable because they encroach
upon the limited area of more important interests. But implicit
in the history of the First Amendment is the rejection of obscenity as utterly without redeeming social importance. This rejection for that reason is mirrored in the universal judgment
that obscenity should be restrained, reflected in the international agreement of over 50 nations, in the obscenity laws of all
of the 48 States, and in the 20 obscenity laws enacted by the
Congress from 1842 to 1956.

The Court defined matter as obscene if "considered as a
whole, its predominant appeal is to prurient interest, i.e., a
shameful or morbid interest in nudity, sex, or excretion, and
if it goes substantially beyond customary limits of candor in
description or representation of such matters." Books such
as *Tropic of Cancer* and *Fanny Hill* were cleared by the
Court, as were countless sordid paperbacks, girlie magazines,
and nude photographs. But in the *Ginzburg* case (383 U.S.
463, 1966) the Court laid down a strange rule: that in a doubtful situation the purveyor could be punished if he advertised
or displayed his material in a way that pandered to prurient
interest. The Court held that evidence of such pandering
might affect its judgment about the character of the material. It found such evidence in the kind of advertising matter
that Ginzburg had sent about his magazine *Eros*, a newsletter
Liaison, and a short book called *The Housewife's Handbook on
Selective Promiscuity*, and in the fact that an attempt had
been made to mail the magazine from the post offices of In-
tercourse and Blue Ball, Pennsylvania, and that it had in fact
been mailed from Middlesex, New Jersey. Justice Brennan
said:

Rather, the fact that each of these publications was created or

35

exploited entirely on the basis of its appeal to prurient interests strengthens the conclusion that the transactions here were sales of illicit merchandise, not sales of constitutionally protected matter.

It should be noted that Justices Black and Douglas have consistently objected to the Court's approach on the ground that the Constitution forbids any restriction on expression. Justice Harlan has approved state, but not federal, prosecutions on the theory there should be room for different attitudes in different parts of the country.

In June 1973 the Court handed down a number of 5-4 decisions which modified earlier ones. The majority rejected the view previously expressed that no material could be prosecuted unless "utterly" without social importance, stating that such importance must be "serious." It also rejected the belief, derived from earlier opinions, that the manner of expression was to be judged by national standards. The new decision left each state free to apply its own standards. But the Court ruled that state laws must specifically define what acts or kinds of expression were to be banned as obscene.

Anyone who participates in the creation or distribution of material found to be obscene can be prosecuted: the author, printer, publisher, seller, or any employee of these. But a person cannot be prosecuted for selling printed matter unless there is proof of some kind that he should have been aware of the nature of the material. So a Los Angeles ordinance was held unconstitutional because it did not require such proof. Justice Brennan said (361 U.S. 147, 1959):

If the contents of bookshops and periodical stands were restricted to material of which their proprietors had made an inspection, they might be depleted indeed. The bookseller's limitation in the amount of reading material with which he could familiarize himself, and his timidity in the face of his absolute criminal liability, thus would tend to restrict the public's access to forms of the printed word which the State could not constitutionally suppress directly. The bookseller's self-censorship, compelled by the State, would be a censorship affecting the whole public, hardly less virulent for being privately administered. Through it, the distribution of all books, both obscene and not obscene, would be impeded.

Of course, the required knowledge (or *scienter*, as the lawyers call it) can be proved by circumstantial evidence. So far the Supreme Court has not reversed a conviction because of the insufficiency of such evidence.

In 1969 the Court unanimously held that it was unconstitutional to prosecute an adult for the private possession of material, however obscene. Justice Marshall said (394 U.S. 557):

But we think that mere categorization of these films as "obscene" is insufficient justification for such a drastic invasion of personal liberties guaranteed by the First and Fourteenth Amendments. Whatever may be the justification for other statutes regulating obscenity, we do not think they reach into the privacy of one's own home. If the First Amendment means anything, it means that a State has no business telling a man, sitting alone in his own house, what books he may read or what films he may watch. Our whole constitutional heritage rebels at the thought of giving government the power to control men's minds.

In May 1971 the Supreme Court ruled that the sender of obscene material through the mails could be punished even if the material was sent to a person who wanted it for his own use and that obscene matter could not be imported into the United States, regardless of its intended use. Justices Black and Douglas dissented in the first case; they were joined by Justice Marshall in the second.

Several states have enacted laws restricting the sale to persons under sixteen (in some cases seventeen or eighteen) of material that would not be considered obscene if sold to an adult, but which offended to some lesser degree. A New York law that embodied the three criteria described above but related them to the young was upheld by the Court.

Most prosecutions for the sale or exhibition of obscene material involve seizure of it under warrants.

In 1961 the Supreme Court held invalid certain procedures provided for by law in Missouri. There a police officer filed a complaint that certain distributors of magazines kept obscene publications for sale. The judge issued search warrants without seeing the supposedly obscene material or giving the distributors an opportunity to contest the claim of obscenity. Police officers then seized a quantity of material. Two months later the Court found that 100 of the publications were obscene but 180 were not. Approximately 11,000 copies were seized at six places. Justice Brennan condemned the issuance of the warrants "on the strength of the conclusory assertions of a single officer, without any scrutiny by the judge of any materials considered by the complainant to be obscene" and also on the ground that the warrants gave police officers complete discretion as to what publications they could seize (367 U.S. 717). In a later case the absence of an "adversary hearing" before seizure was stressed.

These cases have been relied on as holding that no warrant can be constitutionally issued without giving the person charged an opportunity to persuade the judge to whom the prosecutor has applied for the warrant that the material is not obscene. Many federal courts have held that such an adversary hearing is essential but the Supreme Court, agreeing with most state courts, ruled in 1973 that it is not.

In early 1971 the Supreme Court refused to review a federal court decision that had condemned the seizure of underground college newspapers without a search warrant or a prior hearing.

A contention that there can be no arrest for obscenity without a similar hearing with regard to the nature of the material was rejected in 1970 when the Supreme Court affirmed, though without opinion, a lower-court decision to that effect.

Movies have presented problems different from those of printed matter because of the fact that they are exhibited to large audiences. Many states and local communities have required that movies be licensed. In 1915 the Supreme Court upheld this practice on the theory that movies were spectacles rather than organs of public opinion. In 1952 it changed its mind. But the licensing of movies is still permissible provided certain safeguards are guaranteed. In 1965 the Supreme Court in the *Freedman* case (380 U.S. 51) laid down guidelines. Under Maryland law a person was required to submit to a Board of Censors a film he intended to show. If the board disapproved a film as obscene the exhibitor had the right to require the board to reconsider; if it persisted in its opinion, he could appeal to the courts. The law contained no provision for speedy action either by the board or by the courts. The Supreme Court found this to be objectionable. It ruled that any licensing law must require that if a licensing authority believes that a movie is obscene, it has the responsibility to seek a judicial determination. It cannot simply withhold a license and thus impose on the exhibitor the burden of going to court to get one. Moreover, there must be provision in the law for prompt decision by the court.

The Court ruled that New York could not ban *The Miracle* on the ground it was sacrilegious, or *Lady Chatterley's Lover* on the ground it made immorality seem desirable. It also upheld exhibition of *The Lovers* and *The Game of Love*. A Dallas ordinance that permitted restriction on the showing of movies if they would create the impression in young people that sexual promiscuity or extramarital or abnormal sexual relations were "profitable, desirable, acceptable, respectable, praiseworthy or commonly accepted" was held to be too vague.

As the result of a publishing accident the Court, in 1971, failed to pass on the question whether the motion picture *I*

Am Curious (Yellow) was obscene. The Court divided evenly, with Justice Douglas abstaining. That abstention was due to the circumstance that Grove Press, which sponsored the movie, had published some of Justice Douglas' writings in one of its magazines. But for that fact, the motion picture would probably have been cleared, for Justice Douglas' views on obscenity are well known to be liberal. As it is, a state decision banning the picture stands—just as a state decision clearing it is likely to stand by the same vote.

A New York law that prohibited sale to persons under eighteen of material that would appeal to their lust was also found too vague. But a later law was upheld which banned material exhibiting naked breasts, buttocks, or private parts provided it appealed to prurient interest, was patently offensive, and was "utterly" without social importance for minors. (For the role of the Post Office in restricting material alleged to be obscene, see section 1t.)

1d. *Contempt of Court*

You can freely criticize judges outside of court.
You cannot disrupt judicial proceedings by threats.
Uncertainty exists with regard to the extent of punishment for repeated acts.

There is one branch of government, the judiciary, that has proved very sensitive to criticism and has the awesome power of contempt to chastise an offender with. Slowly the Supreme Court has prescribed limits on that power. It has held that a judge could punish for contempt only if there was a clear and present danger that the remarks objected to would obstruct the judicial process. That rule was laid down in a case affecting the West Coast longshoreman leader Harry Bridges. He had sent a telegram to Frances Perkins, then President Franklin Roosevelt's Secretary of Labor, in which he criticized a judge in California for issuing an injunction and threatened that if it was continued in force there might be a strike. His conviction for contempt was set aside. Justice Black said (314 U.S. 252, 1941):

> For these reasons we are convinced that the judgments below result in a curtailment of expression that cannot be dismissed as insignificant. If they can be justified at all, it must be in terms of some serious substantive evil which they are designed to avert. The substantive evil here sought to be averted has been variously described below. It appears to be double: disrespect for the judiciary; and disorderly and unfair administration of justice. The assumption that respect for the judiciary can be won by shielding judges from published criticism wrongly appraises the character of American public opinion. For it is a prized American privilege to speak one's mind, although not always with perfect good taste, on all public institutions. And an enforced silence, however limited, solely in the name of preserving the dignity of the bench, would probably engender resentment, suspicion, and contempt much more than it would enhance respect.

While we are here concerned only with contempt charges based on statements critical of the judiciary, not with charges based on obstructive conduct, principles have evolved in some of the cases in the latter category which also affect cases involving speech. The Supreme Court has circumscribed the power of a judge to try the contempt charge alone. He may do so if the sentence imposed is not greater than six months; otherwise there must be a jury trial. That means that the judge must decide at the outset whether he will impose a sentence of more than six months; if so, he must impanel a jury.

The Court also decided that a judge who was emotionally involved in the controversy which produced the charge of contempt should not try the charge of contempt himself. So

in the case known as the Chicago Seven, in which Judge
Julius Hoffman convicted several defendants and their lawyers of contempt, the government attorney asked the appeals
court to give them all a new hearing before a different judge,
believing that the Supreme Court decision required this. The
Court of Appeals granted that request and sent the contempt
charges for hearing before a different judge. It also ruled
that Judge Hoffman had no right to impose sentences which
totaled more than six months by the device of multiplying
instances of contempt. At the new hearing the government
agreed that the maximum penalty could not exceed six months.

There are two ways in which contempt proceedings can be
initiated; by the judge summarily pronouncing judgment, as
was done in the case of the Chicago Seven, or by requiring the
person charged to show cause, after a hearing, why he should
not be punished. The first procedure is permitted only when
the act complained of has occurred in the judge's presence;
the second when, as in the case of the Bridges telegram, it has
not. (For related information on contempt see also section 42.)

1e. *Distribution of Leaflets*

*You can freely distribute noncommercial leaflets in public
places.*
*You cannot attempt distribution by ringing doorbells on
dwelling places with signs forbidding it.*

The First Amendment protects not only the speaker or
writer, but also the distributor. We have already seen how
this applies, in the area of obscenity, to the bookseller and
motion-picture exhibitor (see section 1c).

The basic principle was first established in 1939 in what are
known as the Leaflet Cases. These involved various ordinances that banned all leaflet distribution. They were challenged by Jehovah's Witnesses. The municipal authorities

sought to sustain the ordinances on the theory that they were aimed at street littering rather than expression of opinion. But the Supreme Court rejected that argument. Justice Roberts laid down a broad rule (308 U.S. 147).

> In every case, therefore, where legislative abridgement of the rights is asserted, the courts should be astute to examine the effect of the challenged legislation. Mere legislative preferences or beliefs respecting matters of public convenience may well support regulation directed at other personal activities, but be insufficient to justify such as diminishes the exercise of rights so vital to the maintenance of democratic institutions.

One aspect of leaflet distribution arose from the practice of Jehovah's Witnesses ringing doorbells and soliciting contributions (and also of people trying to sell magazine subscriptions). The Supreme Court ruled that this practice could not be entirely prohibited. But if a householder indicates that he does not want to be disturbed, a solicitor who persists in ringing the bell can be prosecuted. Ordinarily a notice placed near the householder's doorbell to the effect that peddlers and solicitors are not wanted should suffice.

The protection of distribution was extended to prohibit the imposition of a flat license tax on distribution, even if money was solicited by the distributor, whether he was an itinerant or resident of the community, whether or not he earned his living by his activities. So long as he is a purveyor of ideas he is protected. Freedom to express ideas is not "reserved for those with a large purse." This rule has been applied to activities on private property which is widely open to the public, such as a company-owned town or an army post open to the public. But a municipality can prohibit all distribution of commercial leaflets or advertising matter on its streets. On the other hand, the Supreme Court held in 1971 that distribution cannot be barred when a leaflet attacks the commercial practices of a person.

1f. *Outdoor Meetings*

You can freely talk to others on the streets.
You cannot talk at a place or time that would result in ob-
struction of traffic.

One aspect of free speech is the right to hold meetings on
the streets or in parks. The Supreme Court has never decided
that there is an absolute right to call a meeting in a park. But
it has held that if a community has allowed use of a park, it
may not discriminate between applicants.

So when an ordinance is passed which requires a permit to
hold a street meeting, it must set up reasonable standards for
the exercise of authority by the official responsible. Many convictions of persons who had spoken at street corners without
getting permits have been set aside because the particular ordinances left the decision to an official who had arbitrary
power. It has been held improper to deny a permit to a person
because he had on earlier occasions used language which
might have been punished as a breach of the peace.

It is important to bear in mind, however, that a person who
speaks without having first applied for a permit and without
having gone to court to compel the issuance of the permit
runs the risk of having his conviction affirmed. If the Supreme Court decides that the particular law or ordinance set
up appropriate standards, defiance of it can be punished.
Only, therefore, when it is clear that the official charged with
issuing permits is given arbitrary authority under the ordinance is it safe to defy the law and proceed to talk.

An attempt by the town of Princess Anne, Maryland, to
prevent a meeting of the National States Rights Party because its speakers had used insulting and threatening language directed at Negroes and Jews failed by reason of procedural defects. The municipality had obtained an injunction
without giving the persons affected any notice or opportunity
to resist it. Therefore those who held the meeting despite the

injunction could not be punished for contempt. The Court indicated that the community's interest would better be served by criminal prosecution for anything said that might be unlawful rather than by forbidding the meeting.

1g. *Marches and Parades*

You cannot parade without a permit where one is required unless the ordinance gives arbitrary power to an official to refuse one.

A time-honored way of expressing one's beliefs is to parade. Before the days of radio and television, torchlight parades in support of particular candidates for political office were common in large cities before election day. Patriotic parades, as on Memorial Day, and Mummers' parades, as in New Orleans at Mardi Gras, are well-established institutions. Various ethnic groups parade, often in colorful costume: the Irish on St. Patrick's Day, the Germans in honor of Baron von Steuben, the Poles in honor of Pulaski, the Italians on Columbus Day, to mention only a few. These occasions are so well recognized they create no legal problems.

But suppose a group meets to parade for some cause that is unpopular. Can it do so without seeking permission from the authorities? That depends primarily on local law. There is no doubt that communities have the right to impose restrictions, in the interest of traffic control and public safety. But, as in the case of meetings in public places or parks (see section 1f), the authorities may not discriminate and may not be arbitrary.

Many years ago the Supreme Court unanimously ruled that a community might require a permit for a parade provided the standards by which it judged requests were appropriate to the regulation of public order and did not interfere with freedom of expression. So it is not safe to parade in a place where such a law exists without trying to get a permit and, if it is denied, going to court to review the denial.

But when is a parade not a parade? A distinction appears to exist between marches on sidewalks and those in the street itself. At least the Supreme Court has indicated in a number of cases that persons could not be charged with disorderly conduct for peacefully walking in groups on a sidewalk where there was no local ordinance that required a permit for such walking. Of course such persons might be convicted for obstructing traffic or for refusal to disperse after having been ordered to do so by a policeman in a situation which justified such an order.

1h. *Demonstrations*

You can peaceably demonstrate in any public place.
You cannot use a place unsuitable for demonstrations, such as a jailyard.

Demonstrations are inherently forms of expression and are often interfered with because of hostility toward the objectives of the demonstrators. However, most of the cases which reached the Supreme Court were decided on due process rather than First Amendment grounds; that is, on the absence of facts justifying conviction on the particular charges made.

The "sit-in" and "freedom ride" demonstrations at lunch counters and similar places of public accommodation resulted in prosecutions for disorderly conduct and for trespass. At the 1960 term the Court reversed Louisiana convictions for disorderly conduct on the ground that there was no evidence of illegal conduct. It also reversed convictions of Negroes for playing basketball in a park on the ground that no legal reasons had been advanced to justify the arrests. Trespass convictions were set aside on the ground that a statute which

defined trespass as an entry into premises after warning
could not apply to a person whose original entry was lawful.

In *Cox* v. *Louisiana* the Court reversed three convictions in
two separate opinions. Cox was convicted for disturbing the
peace, obstructing public passages, and picketing a court-
house—the last two in violation of specific statutes. The arrests arose from a peaceful demonstration protesting other
arrests of civil rights workers. Justice Goldberg said that fear
that hostile bystanders might resort to violence did not justify charging the demonstrators with breach of the peace. He
also held that the statute was too vague since it might justify
prosecution merely for the peaceful expression of unpopular
views.

The obstruction conviction was reversed because the law
had not been enforced in other situations where, as here, "arrangements" had been made for parades. The Court recognized, however, that some regulation of parades was permissible.

On the picketing charge the Court upheld the statute, rejected an argument that no "clear and present danger" of
public harm had been shown by the prosecution, but reversed
the convictions on the ground that the state officials had permitted the demonstration across the street from the court-
house and that the later order to disperse rested on the erro-
neous belief there had been a breach of the peace.

Following these decisions the Court reversed convictions
for breaches of the peace where the evidence showed only
that defendants had sat quietly in a branch library to protest
its practice of discrimination. The Court also set aside convictions of peaceful civil rights demonstrators in Chicago despite
the claim by the state's highest court that they had been convicted for refusal to obey a police order to disperse, because
they had not been charged with such failure.

But the Court upheld convictions of demonstrators for refusing to leave a jailyard on the ground that this was not a
suitable place for a demonstration.

47

1i. *Picketing*

You can picket peaceably so long as you do not obstruct.
You cannot picket for an illegal objective.

Picketing to inform the public of the existence of a controversy has had a long history in the field of labor relations. Attempts to curb it entirely were struck down by the Supreme
Court in 1940 on the ground that peaceful picketing was a
form of expression protected by the First Amendment. This
right to picket is not confined to labor unions. Any group has
the right to express its views in this manner so long as it does
not interfere with the rights of others. So peaceful picketing
of an employer against racial discrimination cannot be interfered with. And pickets are to be found in many places expressing the most varied opinions. One man will carry a sign
protesting a particular court decision as unfair to him; another will proclaim the end of the world.

But if the picketing, however peaceful, is for a purpose that
conflicts with some valid local policy, then it can be restricted.
So, in a state which requires employers to bargain only with
representatives of a majority of the workers, picketing by a
union representing a minority for the purpose of compelling
the employer to bargain with it could be enjoined. Thus an injunction against picketing was upheld where a union tried to
get a parking-lot owner who had no employees to conform to
the union's policy with regard to closing hours on the ground
that the state had a right, through its courts, to announce a
policy of protecting the independence of self-employers.

An interesting case arose some years ago in New York. The
state court enjoined picketing on the ground that the signs
contained false statements. The Supreme Court unanimously
ruled this impermissible. Justice Frankfurter said (320 U.S.
293, 1943):

> to use loose language or undefined slogans that are part of the
> conventional give-and-take in our economic and political contro-
> versies—like 'unfair' or 'fascist'—is not to falsify facts.

1j. *The Use of Loudspeakers*

We are all well aware of, and often annoyed by, the use of loudspeakers. Some years ago there were two conflicting 5 to 4 decisions by the Supreme Court within a year of each other. In the first the Court held an ordinance unconstitutional because it gave a police chief unlimited discretion. In the second it upheld an ordinance that prohibited the use of sound trucks making "loud and raucous noises." The Court has not, however, indicated what criteria should be used for determining when noises are of that character. Whether it would uphold an ordinance which banned the use of transistor radios in all public places remains uncertain.

1k. *Maintaining Anonymity*

Throughout our history anonymity has played an important role, especially during times of excitement. From time to time, attempts have been made to require the disclosure of the authors or publishers of anonymous material. The Supreme Court had two occasions to consider such attempts. It refused to pass on a New York ordinance limited to election material because the issue had ceased to have current vitality, the particular election involved having passed. But it struck down a Los Angeles ordinance that forbade distribution of anonymous handbills. Justice Black said (362 U.S. 60, 1960):

> Anonymous pamphlets, leaflets, brochures and even books have played an important role in the progress of mankind. Persecuted groups and sects from time to time throughout history have been able to criticize oppressive practices and laws either anonymously or not at all. The obnoxious press licensing law of England, which was also enforced on the Colonies was due in part to the knowledge that exposure of the names of printers, writers and distributors would lessen the circulation of litera-

ture critical of the government. The old seditious libel cases in England show the lengths to which government had to go to find out who was responsible for books that were obnoxious to the rulers. John Lilburne was whipped, pilloried and fined for refusing to answer questions designed to get evidence to convict him or someone else for the secret distribution of books in England. Two Puritan Ministers, John Penry and John Udal, were sentenced to death on charges that they were responsible for writing, printing or publishing books. Before the Revolutionary War colonial patriots frequently had to conceal their authorship or distribution of literature that easily could have brought down on them prosecutions by English-controlled courts. Along about that time the Letters of Junius were written and the identity of their author is unknown to this day. Even the Federalist Papers, written in favor of the adoption of our Constitution, were published under fictitious names. It is plain that anonymity has sometimes been assumed for the most constructive purposes.

11. *Failure to Register or File Reports*

That a registration requirement can be a restriction of freedom of expression was recognized by the Supreme Court in 1945 when it struck down a Texas requirement that a labor leader must register as an organizer before he could make a speech. But it has not extended that doctrine to a situation where more was involved than speech.

There is a kind of government impingement on the individual that has multiplied in recent years and been challenged on First Amendment grounds: the requirement that people register or make reports. Some of these, such as income tax reports, are beyond challenge. Others have met varying fates.

Congress, in its desire to restrict the activities of the Communist party, created the Subversive Activities Control Board with power to declare organizations as Communist-dominated and require them to register. Its first target obviously was the Communist party itself. The Court upheld the

requirement that the party register, but when the party refused to do so the Court of Appeals for the District of Columbia Circuit set aside its conviction on the ground that anyone
who would have had to sign the necessary document would
have had the right to refuse on the ground that signing might
have incriminated him. And the Supreme Court refused to review.

The Board's findings with regard to a number of other organizations were set aside on the ground that the evidence relied on dealt with too remote a past. Only Justice Black expressed his belief that the law was unconstitutional.

Other situations in which reports are required raise no
First Amendment issues and are discussed in the section dealing with self-incrimination (see section 37).

A curious situation arose in Rhode Island. In an endeavor
to restrict the distribution of obscene material a state commission was established with the power to notify booksellers
and police chiefs that it had found certain books and magazines objectionable for sale to persons under eighteen. As a
result many bookstores withdrew those items from sale. The
Supreme Court did not pass on the constitutionality of this
law but characterized as censorship the way in which the
commission had acted. There was a suggestion in the opinion,
however, that law enforcement officers might express their
views about material offered for sale privately to those concerned. Justice Brennan said (372 U.S. 58, 1963):

> The procedures of the Commission are radically deficient.
> They fall far short of the constitutional requirements of govern-
> mental regulation of obscenity. We hold that the system of in-
> formal censorship disclosed by this record violates the Four-
> teenth Amendment.
> In holding that the activities disclosed on this record are con-
> stitutionally proscribed, we do not mean to suggest that private
> consultation between law enforcement officers and distributors
> prior to the institution of a judicial proceeding can never be con-

stitutionally permissible. We do not hold that law enforcement officers must renounce all informal contacts with persons suspected of violating valid laws prohibiting obscenity. Where such consultation is genuinely undertaken with the purpose of aiding the distributor to comply with such laws and avoid prosecution under them, it need not retard the full enjoyment of First Amendment freedoms. But that is not this case. The appellees are not law enforcement officers; they do not pretend that they are qualified to give or that they attempt to give distributors only fair legal advice. Their conduct as disclosed by this record shows plainly that they went far beyond advising the distributors of their legal rights and liabilities. Their operation was in fact a scheme of state censorship effectuated by extralegal sanctions; they acted as an agency not to advise but to suppress.

1m. *Maintaining Silence*

Does the First Amendment protect a person who refuses to express himself, as it does the person who is eager to expound his views? That question has arisen in a number of contexts: an applicant for a public job refuses to take an oath that would require him to deny certain beliefs and associations; a witness before some investigating body refuses to answer questions about these matters. The Supreme Court has given no clear-cut answer.

On the whole, the witnesses charged with contempt for refusing to answer questions have lost out. In a few cases the Court reversed convictions on nonconstitutional grounds, such as that the particular investigating body had failed to follow its own rules of procedure. But the Court rejected the basic argument that the First Amendment prohibited inquiry for the sake of exposing the witness to being shunned in his community or losing his job or means of livelihood. While the Court had, in the *Watkins* case, stated that no committee of the Congress had the power to inquire merely to expose, it later ruled in *Barenblatt* that the Court would not inquire into the actual motivation of such committee in asking particular questions.

Only in the *Sweezy* case (354 U.S. 234, 1957) did the Court set aside a conviction for refusal of a professor to answer questions about his classroom activities, a majority of the justices basing their ruling on First Amendment grounds (see section 1p for fuller discussion).

Those who rejected oaths were generally more successful, but usually on the ground that the scope of the oath was too broad or its terms too vague (see section 1q).

There are a few special situations in which a person cannot be forced to talk. They derive not from any constitutional principle but from statutes. But these statutes give the right of silence not to protect the person being questioned, but to protect someone else. And that other person can waive his protection. Thus lawyers, doctors, and ministers cannot be forced to tell what they may have confidentially learned from client, patient, or parishioner.

Reporters in various media have, however, claimed the right not to disclose the sources of their information. That situation, obviously, is quite different from the cases we have just discussed. In those it is the matter itself that is kept secret, not the identity of the informant. But the reporter has published the matter, yet wants to hide the identity. This attitude is justified in the name of freedom of the press on the ground that the press could not freely function if informants were identified. In too many situations they would not talk if their anonymity were not protected. The public would no doubt get less information, particularly about political matters. But a defendant's right to a fair trial may be affected if a reporter refuses to disclose the names of persons who might be favorable witnesses. And, of course, the opposite might be true: a prosecution could be prejudiced.

Generally the courts have rejected the reporter's claims. Many have gone to prison for short contempt terms rather

53

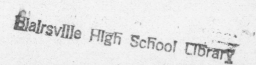

than violate the confidence imposed on them. A few states, however, have given reporters a limited protection.

In November 1970 the United States Court of Appeals for the Ninth Circuit upheld the contention of Earl Caldwell, a Negro reporter for *The New York Times*, that he should not be required to testify before a federal grand jury investigating the Black Panthers unless the government could demonstrate "a compelling need" for his attendance. The decision rested primarily on the sensitivity of the Black Panther situation and Mr. Caldwell's claim that he had won the confidence of the group that would be lost if he were required to testify about it in secret. In June 1972 the Supreme Court reversed that decision by a 5-4 vote and held that a reporter has no constitutional right to refuse to divulge his sources when that information is relevant to an inquiry by a grand jury.

1n. *Defamation*

You can make even false statements about a public person as long as you do not act in reckless disregard of the truth.
You cannot falsely defame anyone not in the public eye.

It was long supposed that the First Amendment in no way protected a person who slandered or libeled another. The theory was that there was no public interest in defamation. But in 1964 that view changed as a result of a case involving *The New York Times.*

The *Times* had accepted and published an advertisement critical of police behavior in a Mississippi town. The police chief of that town, although not named in the advertisement, sued for libel, and succeeded in getting a verdict of $500,000, which was upheld by the state's highest court. The United States Supreme Court reversed this decision and laid down a rule that has had far-reaching effects. No public official, the Court said, could recover for defamation, however false the matter complained of, unless he could show that it was ut-

tered in reckless disregard for the truth. Justice Brennan said
(376 U.S. 254):

> The constitutional guarantees require, we think, a federal
> rule that prohibits a public official from recovering damages for
> a defamatory falsehood relating to his official conduct unless he
> proves that the statement was made with "actual malice"—that
> is, with knowledge that it was false or with reckless disregard
> of whether it was false or not.

The philosophy behind the decision was the importance of
letting the public know everything about its officials. A press
that could be sued if it turned out it had made an honest mis-
take would naturally hesitate before printing anything that
was controversial. The new rule served the public interest. It
was soon extended to cover persons, such as actors, or candidates for public office, who, though not public officials, had entered the public arena. It was applied also to the rare prosecutions for criminal libel.

That was decided in a case involving James Garrison, the
colorful district attorney of Orleans Parish, Louisiana, who
later received much notoriety because of his attempt to establish that a conspiracy had been involved in the assassination
of President Kennedy. He had a dispute with eight judges of
his parish in the course of which he issued a statement charging them with inefficiency, with laziness, and with refusing,
because of sympathy with vice, to authorize the expenditure
of funds to fight it. He was then charged with criminal libel
and convicted. The Supreme Court reversed this conviction,
applying the rule of the *Times* case.

In early 1971 the Court unanimously extended the rule of
The New York Times case to cover publications that incor-
rectly reported charges of criminal behavior by public officials
and candidates for public office, even though the charges did
not relate to official conduct or political activity, on the
ground that any criminal conduct was relevant to the fitness

of such a person to hold public office. Finally, in June 1971, the Court decided to apply the rule of *The New York Times* case to all persons who became involved in any matter of public concern, regardless of their public or private status. As Justice Brennan noted, that rule should obtain "whether the persons involved are famous or anonymous." Justices Harlan, Stewart, and Marshall dissented.

The New York Times rule has had an unexpected bad result. A public person falsely defamed has lost the opportunity of vindicating himself except in the relatively rare instances in which he can establish the reckless disregard of the truth required under the rule. Some mechanism should be devised by which the tribunal could find the defamatory statement false but assess no damages in cases where, under the present rule, the complaint would have to be merely dismissed for lack of proof that the statement was recklessly made. While such a rule might subject newspapers to the expense of defense on the issue of falsity, it would not subject them to the hazards of punitive damages. So far nothing has been attempted in that direction.

There is one rather special aspect of this subject. In an attempt to lessen the consequences of racial and religious prejudice some states have passed what are loosely called group libel laws. These punish anyone who exposes a person "to contempt, derision, or obloquy" because of "race, color, creed or religion." The usefulness of such laws is open to serious question, partly because of the possible boomerang effect of the acquittal of some apostle of hate. That could easily be interpreted as proof that the vile matter purveyed was true. But the Supreme Court has upheld at least one such law, which was enacted in Illinois in an effort to check race riots.

1o. *Invasion of Privacy*

The extent to which a person is protected against the publication of matters relating to his private life varies from state to state. In some states statutes control such activities, in some the courts have worked out a measure of protection, in others the right to protection is not recognized at all. In most states the right of privacy does not extend to a subject that is one of general public interest. If it is, there is no recovery except for defamation (see section 1n). Otherwise, the person affected can enjoin the use of the material and get money damages.

But if the person discussed is a public officer or has become a public figure by his activities, then a different rule has recently been applied on the theory that there is a public interest in learning all the facts about such persons. In other words, the right of freedom of expression overbalances the individual's right of privacy. So the Supreme Court has applied the rule of the *Times* case that redress can be obtained in such situations only if it can be shown that the publication was made in reckless disregard of the truth.

The first application of this rule was in the *Hill* case. There a New York jury had awarded substantial damages against the magazine *Life* because of an article written in 1955 about a sensational occurrence in the Hill family three years earlier that had been recalled to public notice by a novel and a play both called *The Desperate Hours*. Three escaped convicts had taken refuge in the Hill home and held the family as hostages for a period of nineteen hours. While in fact no one had been harmed, the *Life* magazine article said there had been some physical violence and that the daughter of the house had been subjected to a verbal sexual insult. The Supreme Court set the verdict aside because the jury had not been charged in accordance with the principle of the *New York Times* case.

An interesting case involving the conflict between First Amendment rights and the right of privacy was raised in a case which the Supreme Court refused to review despite a dissenting opinion by Justice Harlan, concurred in by Justices Douglas and Brennan. The case arose out of a decision by Massachusetts' highest court which enjoined the commercial showing to general audiences of a film called *Titticut Follies*.

1p   Rights to Personal Freedom

That film was a documentary of life in a Massachusetts hospital for the criminally insane. The state had brought suit on behalf of the inmates to protect their right of privacy.

No principle has yet emerged to protect people from the nuisance of unsolicited telephone calls or the blare of transistors in public places. Legislation which regulated these would probably be upheld. In 1952 the Supreme Court refused to ban music, commercials, and announcements piped into buses in the District of Columbia. It held that the action of the local Public Service Commission, which had approved the project, was within the power given to it by Congress and that no First Amendment rights were violated since no "objectionable propaganda" had been piped.

1p. *Academic Freedom*

Although there is nothing in the Constitution about education, the idea has grown that teachers and even students have certain rights to freedom of expression. Paradoxically the Supreme Court's first contact with education was on behalf of parents.

The antagonism toward the Germans which arose from World War I led to various state laws which restricted teaching. One of these, in Nebraska, prohibited the teaching of all foreign languages; another, in Oregon, forbade all private schools. The Supreme Court struck them both down as an unreasonable interference with the right of parents and guardians to direct the education of their children and as an attempt to standardize teaching. In neither case, however, was there any reference to the First Amendment. The constitutional basis for the decisions was the due process clause of the Fourteenth Amendment which the Court interpreted as banning all state laws it considered unreasonable, an attitude which the Court no longer expresses.

A generation later the problem of teachers' rights came before the Court in review of New York's Feinberg Law, which called for periodic checks on teachers in order to ferret out those who might be members of an organization advocating the overthrow of the government by force. At that time the Court upheld the law on the theory that whatever impact it had on the freedom of teachers was the result of their own choice. Only Justices Black and Douglas dissented. The latter emphasized the trend to orthodoxy that would result from the practices called for by the law. He said (342 U.S. 485, 1952):

What happens under this law is typical of what happens in a police state. Teachers are under constant surveillance; their pasts are combed for signs of disloyalty; their utterances are watched for clues to dangerous thoughts. A pall is cast over the classrooms. There can be no real academic freedom in that environment. Where suspicion fills the air and holds scholars in line for fear of their jobs, there can be no exercise of the free intellect. Supineness and dogmatism take the place of inquiry. A "partyline"—as dangerous as the "partyline" of the Communists—lays hold. It is the "party line" of the orthodox view, of the conventional thought, of the accepted approach. A problem can no longer be pursued with impunity to its edges. Fear stalks the classroom. The teacher is no longer a stimulant to adventurous thinking; she becomes instead a pipe line for safe and sound information. A deadening dogma takes the place of free inquiry. Instruction tends to become sterile; pursuit of knowledge is discouraged; discussion often leaves off where it should begin.

But in 1967 the Court reversed itself, though by a 5 to 4 vote. Justice Brennan said (385 U.S. 589):

Our Nation is deeply committed to safeguarding academic freedom, which is of transcendent value to all of us and not merely to the teachers concerned. That freedom is therefore a special concern of the First Amendment, which does not tolerate laws that cast a pall of orthodoxy over the classroom. "The vigilant protection of constitutional freedoms is nowhere more vital than in the community of American schools." The classroom is peculiarly the "marketplace of ideas." The Nation's future depends upon leaders trained through wide exposure to that robust exchange of ideas which discovers truth "out of a multitude of tongues, [rather] than through any kind of authoritative selection."

A few years earlier the Supreme Court had set aside the contempt conviction of one Sweezy. That case arose from a New Hampshire investigation into subversion. A professor of the humanities was convicted of contempt for refusing to answer questions about the Progressive Citizens of America and its successor, the Progressive party, about a lecture he had given at the University of New Hampshire, and about his beliefs. The Supreme Court set that conviction aside on the ground that the state had not shown that such questions were relevant to an inquiry into subversion. Chief Justice Warren pointed out that there had been an invasion of Sweezy's "liberties in the areas of academic freedom and political expression—areas in which government should be extremely reticent to tread." He said (354 U.S. 234, 1957):

> To impose any strait jacket upon the intellectual leaders in our colleges and universities would impair the future of our Nation. No field of education is so thoroughly comprehended by man that new discoveries cannot yet be made. Particularly is that true in the social sciences, where few, if any, principles are accepted as absolutes. Scholarship cannot flourish in an atmosphere of suspicion and distrust.

Justice Frankfurter said in the same case:

> In the political realm, as in the academic, thought and action are presumptively immune from inquisition by political authority. It cannot require argument that inquiry would be barred to ascertain whether a citizen had voted for one or the other of the

two major parties either in a state or national election. Until recently, no difference would have been entertained in regard to inquiries about a voter's affiliations with one of the various so-called third parties that have had their day, or longer, in our political history.

In striking down a Maryland law which required teachers to take an oath that they were not engaged "in one way or another" in an attempt to overthrow the government by force, the Court noted that the overbreadth of the law might "deter the flowering of academic freedom."

In 1968 the Court vacated the dismissal of a schoolteacher who had made statements critical of school officials which the state court had found to have been false. In so doing the Court applied the libel law of the *New York Times* case (see section 1n) that comment in an area of public interest cannot be curbed unless it is established that the comment was made in reckless disregard of the truth.

Rights of students were first recognized in 1969 in setting aside discipline imposed on students who had worn black armbands in protest against the war in Vietnam. Justice Fortas pointed out the nature of the problem (393 U.S. 503):

It does not concern aggressive, disruptive action or even group demonstrations. Our problem involves direct, primary First Amendment rights akin to "pure speech."

The school officials banned and sought to punish petitioners for a silent, passive, expression of opinion, unaccompanied by any disorder or disturbance on the part of petitioners. There is here no evidence whatever of petitioners' interference, actual or nascent, with the school's work or of collision with the rights of other students to be secure and to be let alone. Accordingly, this case does not concern speech or action that intrudes upon the work of the school or the rights of other students.

This excerpt indicates, however, that the Supreme Court would be unlikely to interfere with disciplinary measures

taken to enforce codes of deportment. There have been a
number of decisions of varying import. Some courts have
ruled that school authorities could not insist on short hair;
others have decided that they could. The Supreme Court has
refused to review a number of both kinds of cases, despite dissents by Justice Douglas.

Academic freedom is generally thought of as giving teachers the right to teach the truth as they see it. Many years ago
the right of a state to ban the teaching of evolution was
tested in the famous Scopes trial in Dayton, Tennessee, in
1925. The antagonists there were William Jennings Bryan,
several times Democratic candidate for the Presidency and
Secretary of State under Wilson, and the famous criminal
lawyer Clarence Darrow. Scopes was convicted but the case
did not get to the United States Supreme Court as the state
Supreme Court set the conviction aside on a minor technical
point. But a similar Arkansas law that forbade teaching that
man had "ascended or descended" from other animals was
held to violate freedom of religion as well as freedom of expression by a unanimous Supreme Court in 1969.

One of the problems that has arisen with respect to both
teachers and students relates to the disciplinary procedures
used by school authorities. For this subject, see Due Process
(Section 48).

1q. *Public Employment*

To what extent does a person lose his rights by entering the
public service? Oliver Wendell Holmes, while a member of the
highest court of Massachusetts, said that since a policeman
had no constitutional right to his job his activities could be restricted. That aphorism is no longer wholly true. The Supreme Court has made it clear that there must be a reasonable relation between the restraint imposed and the

necessities of the public service. So the issue of freedom of expression that may be raised in a particular situation cannot be avoided because the person raising the issue happens to be enjoying the privilege of public employment.

There have been various kinds of such restrictions. The commonest is some form of oath. Many such cases have been decided by the Supreme Court. From them the guiding rules may be simply stated:

1. A law that requires an oath promising only adherence to the state and/or federal constitution is good, even if applied to nongovernment employees such as teachers in tax exempt institutions.

2. A law that requires an oath disclaiming engagement in an attempt to overthrow the government by force is good if clear and specific.

3. A law that requires an oath disclaiming various kinds of vaguely defined "subversive" activities is bad.

So an Oklahoma law that required dismissal of teachers who had been members of a "subversive" organization regardless of their knowledge of the character of the organization was struck down. We have already discussed New York's Feinberg Law (see section 1p).

The federal government and some of the states have passed laws forbidding civil service employees to engage in political activities. The Supreme Court has rejected challenges to such laws based on First Amendment grounds, stating that the laws had not been aimed at expression of opinion, only at activity.

After World War II, the government instituted a Loyalty Program, which resulted in many dismissals. The Supreme Court reversed some of these on various grounds without ever reaching First Amendment issues raised in most of them. In a 5 to 4 decision the Court upheld the arbitrary barring of a cafeteria worker from a naval installation on the ground that no imputation of disloyalty was involved.

1r. *Restrictions in Private Industry*

Attempts to get the Supreme Court to review dismissals or
blacklisting by private employers because of Communist
affiliations or invocation of the privilege against self-incrimination have all failed because the First Amendment is a restriction on government only.

There are many interferences with freedom of expression
in private industry, not only by employers but also by unions.
Even the press, radio, and television have been accused of
throttling free expression by their unwillingness to publish
points of view they dislike. To some extent radio and television are limited by the Federal Communications Commission's "fairness" doctrine (see section 1w). But no legal
method has yet been achieved to require the press to print
what it doesn't want to.

1s. *Symbolic Speech*

*Certain acts may be considered a form of expression of opin-
ion and so protected by the First Amendment, but the area is
an uncertain one.*

In 1931 the Court reversed a conviction under a California
law which prohibited the display of a red flag (1) as a symbol
of "opposition to organized government," (2) as a "stimulus to
anarchistic action," (3) as an aid to "seditious" propaganda.
The case arose because the defendant, a member of the
Young Communist League, had children at a camp participate in a daily ceremony at which the flag of Soviet Russia
was raised and a pledge of allegiance to it recited. There was
also evidence that she owned and kept in the camp's library
books and pamphlets that incited to violence and "armed
uprisings." But she testified that none of that material had
been in any way brought to the attention of any child. The

trial judge allowed the jury to convict if it found that the flag was used for any of the three purposes specified in the law. The Supreme Court considered this improper as it allowed the jury to convict even if it found only that the flag had been flown in opposition to government. To permit a conviction on that basis alone, said the Court, would violate the First Amendment's guarantee of freedom of speech.

This case is the first one in which the concept of an act as symbol of speech was accepted. The same principle was later applied to peaceful picketing (see section 1i), to the refusal of the children of Jehovah's Witnesses to salute the flag (see section 3a), to peaceful sit-ins (see 1h), and to the wearing of black armbands by students to protest against the war in Vietnam (see section 1p). It was, however, rejected in the draft-card-burning cases that arose out of hostility to the war in Vietnam.

In 1971, by a 4-4 decision, Justice Douglas abstaining, the Court upheld a New York conviction, under a statute that punishes the desecration of the American flag, of an art dealer who had displayed pieces of sculpture in public that used the flag to represent a penis. No opinion was written, nor was the lineup of the Justices announced. Defendant's claim that the statues were a form of artistic protest protected by the First Amendment thus did not prevail.

In March 1971 the United States Court of Appeals sitting in Washington reversed the conviction of Abbie Hoffman, the Yippie leader, on a charge of defiling the flag by wearing a shirt made in its design when appearing before the House Committee on Un-American Activities.

1t. *Use of the Mails*

Congress has given the Post Office a certain amount of control over matter sent through the mails. Most important to the exercise of First Amendment rights is the control of the

second-class-mailing privilege, vital to newspapers and periodicals. During World War I the Postmaster General revoked
the privilege of the *Milwaukee Leader* because certain of its
issues contained matter hostile to the conduct of the war. The
Supreme Court upheld this action.

In 1946 the Supreme Court ruled against the Postmaster
General when he revoked the privilege of the magazine *Es-
quire* on the ground that its contents were not elevating. The
Court ruled that the law gave the Post Office no power to deal
with such an issue.

In 1958 the Court, without writing any opinions, set aside
Post Office orders which had barred certain periodicals from
the mails as obscene, including one that dealt with homosexual themes. Presumably these decisions rested on findings
that the material was not obscene, rather than on any challenge to the power of the Post Office.

In 1971, however, the Court unanimously struck down two
acts of Congress on the express ground that they interfered
with freedom of expression. One of these laws, passed in the
nineteenth century, authorized the Postmaster General to
block all mail sent to a person who, after a hearing, had been
found to have mailed obscene matter. The other law, passed
in 1950, permitted the Post Office to get a court order block-
ing the mail while the hearing in the Post Office was under
way. The Court held these laws to be unconstitutional because they did not give the persons affected an opportunity
for prompt judicial review of the issue of obscenity. This is in
line with the rules laid down in connection with the licensing
of motion pictures (see section 1c).

The converse of the problem presented by that case has not
yet been considered by the Supreme Court: Can the Post
Office stop anyone from getting mail that he wants to have
because the Post Office has some objection to the mailed item?

The Court held unconstitutional, as an interference with
freedom of expression, an act of Congress which had authorized the Post Office to withhold mail that it considered to be

propaganda material from outside the United States unless
the addressee had specifically requested delivery in writing.

In 1970 the Supreme Court unanimously rejected an attack
on an Act of Congress which permits a person who has received an advertisement offering for sale material which the
addressee believes to be "erotically arousing or sexually provocative" to ask the Postmaster General to issue an order to
the mailer to remove the person's name from its lists and to
stop future mailings. The suit was brought by publishers and
distributors of mail order houses and lists. Chief Justice Burger stressed that a man's home is his castle and that he had
an absolute right to ban unwanted material. He noted also
that no sanctions could be imposed without a hearing.

Another Act of Congress that requires publishers and ad-
vertisers to label all mailings of "sexually oriented" material
and prohibits the mailing of such material to any one who has
been listed by the Postal Service as having indicated that he
does not want such mail is now under attack in the courts.

1u. *Admission to the Bar*

From time to time aspiring lawyers have challenged, on
First Amendment grounds, regulations imposed by the states
for admission to the bar or the application of these laws in
their own cases.

In 1945 the Court held that Illinois could deny admission to
the bar to a pacifist because the state's constitution required
all male adults to perform military service in time of war and
lawyers had to swear to support the constitution. Justices
Black, Douglas, Murphy, and Rutledge dissented.

In 1957 the Supreme Court unanimously decided that a person could not be barred for past membership in the Communist party and that refusal to answer questions about such
membership was not evidence of lack of good moral character. But a few years later the Court decided that refusal to

answer such questions was ground for rejection because the state was entitled to the information even when, as was the situation in another case, there had been no suggestion that the applicant had any Communist connections. In both cases Chief Justice Warren and Justices Black, Douglas, and Brennan dissented.

In February 1971 the Court dealt with this subject in three 5 to 4 decisions. The Court ruled that an Arizona law-school graduate could not be denied the right to practice law merely because she refused to state that she had never belonged to any organization that advocated the overthrow of the government by force, and that an applicant could not be barred by Ohio because he refused to list organizations he had joined. In both those cases Chief Justice Burger and Justices Harlan, White, and Blackmun dissented, in opinions written by Justice Blackmun.

But in the third case Justice Stewart joined these justices in a decision which upheld the right of New York to require applicants to submit proof that they were "loyal" to the government and to state whether they had ever belonged to an organization whose aim was to overthrow the government by force and whether it had been their intent to advance that aim. Justices Black, Douglas, Brennan, and Marshall dissented.

The distinction between the cases which evidently led Justice Stewart to take a more conservative position in the last of those cases was that New York, unlike Arizona and Ohio, allowed for the possibility that membership had not involved acceptance of any illegal aims of the organization.

1v. *The Press*

The Supreme Court has consistently condemned attempts to curb newspaper publication. In 1931 it ruled that a state could not prevent publication of a newspaper because past issues had been scandalous. Later it struck down a Louisiana tax on advertising the purpose of which was to restrict papers having a large circulation.

In June 1971 the Court was confronted with its most important free-press problem. After *The New York Times* and the *Washington Post* had published material gleaned from the secret 1968 McNamara report on Vietnam, the government sued to enjoin further publication on the ground that this would adversely affect national security. The Court by a 6 to 3 vote upheld the right of the newspapers to publish the material. The Court said that there was a heavy presumption against interfering with the press and that the government had not overcome that presumption. Chief Justice Burger and Justices Harlan and Blackmun dissented.

1w. *Miscellaneous Activities*

There have been a few cases that more or less involve freedom of expression but are not susceptible of classification.

An interesting situation arose in Houston, Texas, where a person wore an army uniform while taking part in a street skit protesting the war in Vietnam. He was prosecuted under a federal law making the unauthorized wearing of such a uniform illegal, except when worn by an actor in such a way as not to bring the military into disrepute. This, the Court held in 1970, was an improper restriction. Justice Black said (398 U.S. 58):

An actor, like everyone else in our country, enjoys a constitutional right to freedom of speech, including the right openly to criticize the Government during a dramatic performance. The last clause of §772 (f) denies this constitutional right to an actor who is wearing a military uniform by making it a crime for him to say things which tend to bring the military in discredit and disrepute. . . . The final clause of §772(f), which leaves Americans free to praise the war in Vietnam but can send persons . . .

to prison for opposing it, cannot survive in a country which has
the First Amendment. To preserve the constitutionality of §772
(f) that final clause must be stricken from the section.

The Court unanimously held it was a violation of the First
Amendment for the Georgia legislature to refuse to seat Ju-
lian Bond because he had expressed views hostile to the war
in Vietnam.

The Court reversed the federal conviction of a man who, in
airing his views about Vietnam, said that if he were drafted
he would use his rifle on President Johnson, and the New
York conviction of a man who said he was burning an American flag in protest of the shooting of James Meredith. Both
were 5 to 4 decisions.

The Supreme Court reversed the conviction, under a law
restricting electioneering on election day, of a newspaper editor because he had published an editorial that day urging
adoption of a particular measure before the voters.

In 1958 the Court struck down an attempt by California to
restrict exemption from taxation as interference with freedom of speech. Veterans and churches were denied exemption
from certain taxes because they refused to subscribe to an
oath that they did not advocate the overthrow of the government by force and did not advocate the support of a foreign
government in the event of hostilities. The Court held that
the methods for determining whether persons claiming exemption came within the proscribed class were unduly bur-
densome because the burden was put on the taxpayer.

For many years the Federal Communications Commission
has required that public issues be discussed on radio and television and that each side be given fair coverage. This has
been known as the fairness doctrine. It has been elaborated to
provide for free time to reply when, during such discussion,
an attack is made on personal characteristics of some particular person or group. A book entitled *Goldwater—Extremist on
the Right* was discussed on a radio station. The speaker said of

the book that it was written "to smear and destroy Barry Goldwater." The author asked for free time to reply. The station refused. The FCC then ordered the station to give him that opportunity. The station argued before the Supreme Court that the FCC rule restricted its freedom of expression. The Supreme Court upheld the FCC and pointed out that on the contrary the rule expanded freedom. Justice White said (395 U.S. 367, 1969):

> It is the purpose of the First Amendment to preserve an uninhibited marketplace of ideas in which truth will ultimately prevail, rather than to countenance monopolization of that market, whether it be by the Government itself or a private licensee.

2. Freedom of Association and Assembly

The First Amendment prohibits Congress from passing any law abridging "the right of the people peaceably to assemble, and to petition the Government for a redress of grievances." The latter aspect of this guarantee has caused no real problem. But complications have arisen in fixing the circumstances under which persons can come together. However, the guarantee is not limited to actual gatherings. It extends also to the more intangible right of association.

The Supreme Court did not include the right of assembly among the rights guaranteed against state action through the due process clause of the Fourteenth Amendment until 1937. It then ruled that no one could be prosecuted for speaking at a meeting merely because it had been organized by the Communist party. But a state may punish participation if the assembly is called for the purpose of committing acts of violence.

As we have seen (section 1g), parades can be regulated in the interest of public order.

The extent to which organizations can be required to list the names of their members depends on circumstances. Many years ago the Court upheld a New York law aimed at the Ku Klux Klan which required such listings by all organizations whose members are bound by an oath. But an Alabama law aimed at the NAACP was struck down in 1958 because of the prejudice its members in that state would suffer by public listing. An Arkansas license tax ordinance which required all organizations to list the names of contributors was held unconstitutional because of its impact on freedom of association and the absence of any relevant connection between the names and the objectives of a tax law. Louisiana laws aimed at nonprofit organizations met the same fate, as did an Arkansas law which required teachers in publicly supported schools and colleges to list all organizations to which they had belonged or contributed.

One of the functions of some organizations has been to supply lawyers to their members. A Virginia law prohibiting such service was held void when applied to the NAACP. Later the Court ruled that labor unions could recommend lawyers to their members.

The question of sit-ins has resulted in a number of decisions by the Court, not always easily reconcilable. Convictions in South Carolina of persons who had sat in on the grounds of the state capitol in protest against segregation were set aside on the ground that they had merely exercised their right of assembly in a public place. But convictions of similarly protesting students who refused to leave the grounds of a jail were sustained. Justice Black distinguished between demonstrations on property generally open to the public and on that to which access was properly limited, such as a jail.

Convictions of peaceful demonstrators against segregation in Chicago who refused to disperse when ordered to do so were reversed on the narrow ground that they had been charged with disorderly conduct, not with refusal to obey a police order. The Court pointed out that their activities had been entirely peaceful. It did not, therefore, have to face up to the question whether the police could order such demonstrators to disperse because the police feared violence from bystanders. Justices Black and Douglas pointed out that states could, by narrowly drawn laws, regulate the activities of pickets and demonstrators.

We have already discussed some of the problems that grew out of hostility to the Communist party (see sections 1a, 1p, 1q). New York laws that required teachers to disclaim membership in the party were set aside because of their restriction on freedom of association. So it was held an invasion of that freedom to deny employment in a defense facility merely because of Communist party membership. But the Court indicated that the result would have been different had the law been restricted to employment in sensitive positions.

An interesting extension of the right of association arose in the Connecticut birth control case. Two people, the executive director of the state's Planned Parenthood League and a doctor who acted as medical director for the league, were convicted for giving contraceptive advice to married persons. A Connecticut law punished the use of any drug or article for purposes of preventing conception and another made equally guilty anyone who aided in the commission of such an offense. The Supreme Court reversed the convictions on the ground that the privacy of the association of marriage had been invaded. Justice Douglas said (381 U.S. 479, 1965):

We deal with a right of privacy older than the Bill of Rights
—older than our political parties, older than our school system.
Marriage is a coming together for better or for worse, hopefully
enduring, and intimate to the degree of being sacred. It is an association that promotes a way of life, not causes; a harmony in living, not political faiths; a bilateral loyalty, not commercial or social projects. Yet it is an association for as noble a purpose as any involved in our prior decisions.

3. Freedom of Religion

The First Amendment says that Congress shall make no law "respecting an establishment of religion, or prohibiting the free exercise thereof." The subject of religious freedom has, therefore, two aspects: "free exercise" and "establishment." Most of the early cases dealt with the former aspect, many of the recent ones with the latter. The basic philosophy of the cases has been a requirement that government be "neutral" in dealing with religion.

Like other provisions of the Bill of Rights, the provisions with respect to religion became binding on the states only through the Fourteenth Amendment, and this effect was not recognized until well into the twentieth century.

3a. *Worship*

You can worship as you please.
You cannot justify an illegal act by religious conviction.

Many years ago the Court had upheld convictions of Mormons for practicing polygamy on the ground that religious freedom could not be asserted as justification for action deemed by the legislature to be contrary to public policy. Chief Justice Waite said (98 U.S. 145, 1879):

> Laws are made for the government of action, and while they cannot interfere with mere religious beliefs and opinions, they may with practices.

Problems have arisen when persons holding unconventional beliefs have objected to measures deemed by society to be essential for its safety. The opposition of Jehovah's Witnesses to their children saluting the flag in school was ultimately successful, but the opposition of Christian Scientists to vaccination failed. In a few cases parents have objected to operations which doctors believed essential. The courts have not been sympathetic.

The refusal of Jehovah's Witnesses to permit their children to salute the flag at school ceremonies occasioned later tests of this principle. In some cases the children were expelled from schools; in others, proceedings were taken against the parents. In 1940 the Court, in an opinion written by Justice Frankfurter, gave express approval to state laws requiring schoolchildren to salute the flag. Justice Stone, in solitary dissent, conceded that the guarantee of religious freedom was not absolute, but believed that since methods other than compulsion could be found to teach patriotism and loyalty the state should not use compulsion on persons having religious scruples. Three years later the Court reversed itself. Justice Jackson said that compulsory unification of opinion was contrary to the essential character of our government.

A different problem arose in connection with the Amish. They object to compulsory school education until the age of sixteen, partly because the years fourteen to sixteen are designated by their religion for intensive Bible study and farm training, partly because those are high school years and the subjects taught there are too worldly. Early in 1971 the Wisconsin Supreme Court ruled that the state's interest in compelling education for those two years was not sufficiently great to offset the claims of religious freedom of the Amish parents. The United States Supreme Court unanimously upheld that decision.

The Court in 1961 unanimously struck down a Maryland statute which required all applicants for public office to swear to belief in God on the ground that this was an interference with religious beliefs, or the lack of them.

An attempt by New York City to license street speakers on religious subjects was struck down because the ordinance set up no standards to guide the licensing authority. The Court recognized, however, that some regulation of street meetings dealing with this explosive subject might be permissible.

The Court struck down an Arkansas law that forbade the teaching of the theory—contrary to the biblical story of man's creation—that men had "ascended or descended" from other animals.

A curious aspect of the principle that government must keep its hands off in religious matters arose some years ago. A controversy developed between religious factions over the right to control the Orthodox Russian Cathedral in New York City. One of the contending factions was said to be under the control of the Soviet Government. When it took possession of the cathedral the New York legislature passed a law which transferred possession to the rival faction, supposedly free from the influence of the Soviet Government. But the Supreme Court said this could not be done.

In 1969 the Court applied the principle of that case to a situation which had arisen in Georgia. After a dispute about doctrine had arisen between local Presbyterian churches and the parent organization, the local churches sued to prevent the parent body from interfering with their property, claiming that the parent body had abandoned the original doctrines of the church. The Supreme Court unanimously reversed a verdict in favor of the local group on the ground that the First Amendment forbade any inquiry into religious issues such as the abandonment of doctrine.

3b. *Separation of Church and State*

The troublesome question of aid to church schools has received attention from the Supreme Court several times in recent years. The Court unanimously expressed the opinion that the First Amendment compels the complete separation of church and state and bans direct aid to religion. But it decided that payment of bus fares to parents of parochial-school children was permissible since it was not aid to the school but to the parents. And the Court upheld a New York law which required a school district to buy textbooks for the use of children in parochial schools on the theory that this benefited the children, not the schools.

The Court has condemned a variety of laws which sought to aid private schools by grants for supposedly nonreligious purposes, and for tax credits and tuition refunds to parents, on the ground that they were motivated to assist religious schools. But the Court upheld federal and state grants for building construction at colleges affiliated with religions.

The Court has approved the release of school children from their regular schedules for religious instruction when this was given outside school property, but condemned such release when the instruction was given in the school.

The Supreme Court has held unconstitutional the use in public schools of a prayer prepared by public authority even though any child who objected was allowed to be excused from participation. It also held that the recitation of the Lord's Prayer and Bible reading were forbidden as involving religious matters.

The Court ruled that a state might not deny unemployment insurance to a Seventh Day Adventist who refused to work on Saturday. But the Court rejected First Amendment challenges to various state laws which forbade Sunday sales, even in the case of Orthodox Jews who thus were deprived of two days of business activity. It also rejected a challenge to tax exemption of property used for church purposes.

4. The Right to Privacy

Concern has been voiced over the extent to which the privacy of persons is being invaded by government activities of various kinds. Among these are the accumulation of data in computer banks, surveillance of meetings by police and army intelligence agents, and listings by congressional and legislative committees. No settled legal principles have yet been developed in any of the areas. In one case a lower federal court enjoined the Public Printer from printing or distributing a list of alleged radical speakers at various universities on the ground that its preparation by a congressional committee served no legislative purpose, but it refused to enjoin publication of the list by any congressman. The list was then leaked to the press and published. Surveillance may be easier to stop, but probably not until its objectives have been largely accomplished. To attack the computer will require much ingenuity.

The first case involving protection of privacy which was considered by the Supreme Court grew out of the piping of music, commercials, and occasional announcements in buses in the District of Columbia. The Court refused to stop it, primarily on the ground that the practice had been approved by the Public Service Commission of the District under the power given to it by Congress. The Court rejected the contention that the right of privacy of bus riders had been invaded, noting that by using the buses the riders had, in effect, consented to what the regulatory body found desirable.

Justice Frankfurter abstained from taking part, saying (343 U.S. 451, 1952):

> My feelings are so strongly engaged as a victim of the practice in controversy that I had better not participate in judicial judgment upon it.

Justice Douglas, in dissent, said:

> If liberty is to flourish, government should never be allowed to force people to listen to any radio program. The right of privacy should include the right to pick and choose from competing

entertainments, competing propaganda, competing political philosophies. If people are let alone in those choices, the right of privacy will pay dividends in character and integrity. The strength of our system is in the dignity, the resourcefulness, and the independence of our people. Our confidence is in their ability as individuals to make the wisest choice. That system cannot flourish if regimentation takes hold. The right of privacy, today violated, is a powerful deterrent to any one who would control men's minds.

Justice Black also dissented, but only on the ground that the broadcasting of news, speeches, or opinions violated the First Amendment.

Early in 1971 the Supreme Court struck down a Wisconsin law (a law which exists also in many other states) which provided for the listing in bars of the names of persons believed to be alcoholics. Since no machinery was provided in the law for a hearing which might protect a person from being listed, the Supreme Court held that the law was a denial of due process and an invasion of privacy.

On the other hand the Court found no improper invasion of privacy in a requirement that a welfare recipient allow periodic inspection at reasonable times of his or her home by caseworkers under penalty of losing welfare benefits.

4a. *Searches and Seizures*

Government agents cannot ordinarily search a person or a home without a warrant.

Government agents can search a person and, to a limited extent, the place where he is at the time of a lawful arrest.

If a search is unlawful nothing taken can be used in a criminal prosecution or for the forfeiture of property.

It is an ancient maxim of English law that every man's home is his castle. But a judge can force open the castle by issuing a search warrant. Ordinarily such a warrant must specify the particular property that is to be looked for and taken. But in the late seventeenth century warrants were used in England to ferret out evidence of suspected sedition. Because the authorities did not know what to look for they authorized the searching officer to take whatever he might find. These "general" warrants became roving commissions to seize all the papers found in a suspect's home.

This practice was first challenged in Massachusetts in the eighteenth century after smuggling had developed between the colonies and the West Indies. There they were called writs of assistance. In 1761 James Otis resigned his office of Attorney General of the Massachusetts colony to attack their use. He questioned the power of Parliament to authorize this practice. But the colonial court ruled against him. John Adams later described this episode as the first step on the road to independence.

A few years later this practice was successfully challenged in England by the radical critic of the government John Wilkes in suits for damages against the officers who had seized his papers. The English courts held that such "general warrants" were void and laid down the principle that there could be no search of a man's home at all for papers to be used as evidence, but only for stolen property or other contraband material. The Fourth Amendment to the United States Constitution was adopted to perpetuate both of these aspects of the doctrine established by the English courts:

> The right of the people to be secure in their persons, houses, papers, and effects, against unreasonable searches and seizures, shall not be violated, and no warrants shall issue but upon probable cause, supported by oath or affirmation, and particularly describing the place to be searched and the persons or things to be seized.

The Fourth Amendment assures protection of the privacy of the house and lessens the possibility of oppression or blackmail by public officials. It is significant that the amendment not only requires that certain particulars be observed before any warrant can be issued, but that it also forbids "unreasonable searches." On the whole the Supreme Court has interpreted and applied this guarantee liberally. Certain rules have developed:

1. If you are lawfully arrested the police have a right to search your person and, to a limited extent, the place where you are arrested. A search of the rear room of an apartment was, in 1970, held improper. The theory behind the rule is that you may be carrying a weapon or be in possession either of the fruits of the crime for which you are arrested or the means by which it was accomplished. Of course, if the arrest was illegal then the search will also be illegal.

If an arrest is valid, material found can be used in a prosecution for an offense other than that for which the arrest was made. In December 1973 the Court upheld convictions for possession of narcotics found in packages on persons who had been arrested for traffic violations. Justices Douglas, Brennan, and Marshall dissented on the ground that searches incidental to arrests should be restricted to what is necessary to protect the officer or prevent destruction of evidence of the offense for which the arrest was made.

Earlier the Court had upheld the right of a policeman, even in the absence of an arrest, to stop people and "frisk" them if the circumstances justified the policeman in believing a crime was about to be committed. In an Ohio case the officer stopped and frisked three men he believed to be "casing" a store in preparation for a stickup, and found one of them was carrying a pistol. The conviction on the charge of possessing a concealed weapon was upheld, with only Justice Douglas dissenting. In one New York case the policeman saw a man talk with known narcotics addicts and then take some heroin out of his pocket. The Supreme Court held this search to have been unjustified because there was no basis for any belief that the man was dangerous. In the second case tools commonly used by burglars were taken by an officer who saw two men tiptoeing on the stairway of an apartment house in which the officer lived. The men ran as he slammed the door to his apartment and were caught on the way down. The Supreme Court upheld that conviction. The Court avoided passing on the constitutionality of the New York law. This time Justice Douglas did not dissent.

2. Except in connection with an arrest there can be no search of a dwelling place without a warrant. The warrant must have been issued on the basis of a sworn statement which connects the material to be seized with the place to be searched. Such a statement can rest on information given to the police by an unnamed person provided the police officer vouches for his reliability and to some extent has corroborated the information given. In other words "probable cause" must be shown.

When a health officer sought to inspect premises a warrant was for many years believed unnecessary. In 1967 the Court held otherwise. However, in such a situation it is not necessary to show need for the inspection of the particular building, only that there was a health hazard in the neighborhood.

The question whether inspection by a welfare caseworker of an apartment occupied by a welfare recipient constituted a search was finally decided in the negative by the Supreme Court in January 1971. New York, as well as many other states, requires a welfare recipient to allow periodic inspections in order to check continued eligibility. If the caseworker is refused admittance he can stop the welfare payments. A lower federal court had ruled that this was an impermissible search. The Supreme Court disagreed. Justice Blackmun wrote the majority opinion, his first. Justices Douglas, Brennan, and Marshall dissented, believing that the rule laid down in connection with inspections by health officers should control here.

3. Even if a warrant has been properly obtained, the search may be held illegal if the warrant was not properly executed, as when the officers break in without announcing their au-

thority. And even a warrant will not authorize the ransacking of the premises searched. When the matter to be seized constitutes printed material the warrant must describe it with "the most scrupulous exactitude"; otherwise an officer could act on his own judgment as to what should be taken and seriously impair freedom of expression. The same rule applies to motion pictures. In both cases there must be judicial scrutiny of the material before a warrant can properly be authorized by the judge. Of course if an officer comes to your home and wants to search it, you should insist on getting a copy of the warrant and the affidavit on which it rested and you should give these papers to your lawyer.

4. The rules with regard to moving vehicles such as automobiles, boats, and aircraft are different. The Supreme Court long ago recognized that it was often impractical to get a warrant because, in the meantime, the bird will have flown. So a search of such vehicles without a warrant is proper provided it rests on probable cause, not on mere suspicion.

5. Searches by customs agents are more liberally permitted.

6. For over a century the courts had ruled that only contraband or things that were used in the commission of a crime could be seized even under a warrant. Things merely "evidentiary," such as clothing or diaries, could not. In 1967 the Supreme Court relaxed that rule in regard to clothing found after a "hot pursuit" of a suspect. It left open the important question of the application of the new rule to writings of any kind.

7. The question of who can complain about a search has troubled the courts for a long time. It is now established that anyone can complain if the property was his even if the premises searched were not, or, even without a showing of ownership of the property, if the defendant is charged with possession of it.

8. A search may be upheld even without a warrant if consented to. The consent of a person who has been arrested will

not be lightly inferred. It must be the consent of a person in possession; that of a landlord, for instance, doesn't count.

9. If the search was illegal the fact that contraband or incriminating evidence was discovered does not make it legal. And, under proper procedures, the use of illegally seized material at a criminal trial or in forfeiture proceedings can be prevented.

The material seized, if not contraband such as narcotics, will be returned to the owner. In 1969 the Court held that fingerprints taken during an illegal search could not be used in a criminal trial. The same rule has been applied to statements made by the person searched.

10. The protection afforded by the Fourth Amendment has been applied to state and local seizures since 1961. It applies to all agencies of government.

4b. *Eavesdropping*

The government cannot use information obtained by telephone taps or by electronic eavesdropping except, perhaps, if a court authorizes the practice.

There are many varieties of eavesdropping. There is no way to prevent a person from testifying to what he overheard by the age-old habit of listening at a keyhole or in any other place that is available. But as soon as he uses aids that modern science has developed a different situation may arise, especially if he is a government agent.

The first mechanical aid to eavesdropping was the tapping of telegraph or telephone wires. More than a generation ago the Supreme Court, despite Justice Holmes's characterization of wiretapping as "dirty business," refused to treat it as a violation of the Fourth Amendment. That decision was, however, overrruled in 1967.

In the meantime Congress had made it a criminal offense to

divulge information obtained by tapping wires. And the Supreme Court ruled that such information could not be used in a criminal trial even if the tapping was done by law enforcement agents. At first this rule was applied to federal cases only. But in 1968 it was extended to the states. The practice then developed of having a judge authorize taps for limited periods of time and the Court has, in effect, sanctioned this provided that certain safeguards are observed. But only a person whose conversation has been listened to can object to the use of taps.

For a time it was uncertain to what extent agents of the government could use sensitive microphones attached to the wall of a room to listen in on conversations conducted inside the room. The Supreme Court has now outlawed such practices.

But the Court has approved the use of electric appliances which permit an informer to transmit conversations to waiting agents or to record them.

In 1969 the Court, in a group of cases which included convictions for threats to kill and for espionage, clarified the procedure to be followed when the government admitted that there had been electronic surveillance. The Court rejected the government's contention that the records should be inspected by the judge in private to decide which records were relevant and should be shown to defense counsel. The Court held this did not enable defendants adequately to protect their rights and so remanded the cases for hearings at which it would be determined whether there had been illegal eavesdropping, whether the defendant was so connected with the eavesdropping that he had the right to complain of it, and whether the use of the illegal material contributed to the convictions.

One of the points made by the government was that disclosure of some of the material might be contrary to the national interest. The Court suggested that in such a situation the government might prefer to drop a prosecution rather

than disclose the material. Another point raised by the
government related to surveillance of foreign embassies. The
Court did not pass on that issue. But the Nixon administration has taken the position that electronic surveillance
without prior judicial approval was permissible even with
regard to possible domestic revolutionaries. The Supreme
Court unanimously rejected that contention in 1972.

4c. *Abortion*

Until very recently it had been taken for granted that laws
prohibiting abortions except under very special circumstances
were constitutional. But in the past few years the sentiment
has developed that a woman has the right to do with her body
what she pleases. Several courts have declared the abortion
law of their states unconstitutional on this ground. In some
states the laws have been modified in various ways. In New
York, for example, an abortion is legal if performed by a
licensed physician with the consent of the woman, either to
preserve her life or within twenty-four weeks of the inception
of pregnancy.

In January 1973 the Supreme Court (Justices White and
Rehnquist dissenting) restricted the right of states to regulate abortions. In the first three months of a woman's
pregnancy a state can require only that the operation be
performed by a licensed physician. In the next three months a
state can also regulate the facilities involved. It can restrict
abortions in the last 10 weeks of pregnancy to those required
to preserve the life or health of the mother. The Court
rejected the contention that a fetus is a "person" entitled to
constitutional protection from conception. Justice Blackmun
said (409 U.S. 113):

> . . . the "compelling" point, in the light of present medical
> knowledge, is at approximately the end of the first trimester.
> . . . from and after this point, a State may regulate the

abortion procedure to the extent that the regulation reasonably relates to the preservation and protection of maternal health. . . . prior to this "compelling" point, the attending physician, in consultation with his patient, is free to determine, without regulation by the State, that in his medical judgment the patient's pregnancy should be terminated.

5. Freedom from Involuntary Servitude

Once President Lincoln had abolished slavery as a war measure, it became evident that a successful North would not permit its reintroduction. Even before the Civil War had been won, a constitutional amendment was proposed in the very words of the ordinance of 1787 which had declared that the Northwest Territory should be the abode of free men only. It was ratified December 18, 1865, and became the Thirteenth Amendment:

> Neither slavery nor involuntary servitude, except as a punishment for crime whereof the party shall have been duly convicted, shall exist within the United States, or any place subject to their jurisdiction.

Of all the provisions of the Constitution, this alone is all-embracing. It binds the federal government, the states, and all persons within the confines of the country. In no uncertain terms it announces that slavery in all its forms should be abolished. While prompted by concern for the Negro, this amendment is yet so broad that it covers all persons. Congress has made it a criminal offense to practice peonage. And the Supreme Court has held such legislation to be within the power of Congress under the Thirteenth Amendment.

Nevertheless, persons interested in procuring forced labor

for their plantations adopted various devices to secure their objective. Some plantation owners developed the device of paying fines imposed by the courts on petty offenders and then obtaining agreements from the offenders that they would work for a fixed period. Congress declared such agreements to be in violation of the amendment and the Supreme Court sustained criminal prosecutions based on attempts to enforce such contracts.

Another device adopted by states favoring employers of cheap labor was to pass laws punishing persons who fraudulently obtained money as an advance payment for work. These laws declared that the fraud would be presumed from the failure to complete the work. The Supreme Court repeatedly struck down such laws on the ground that there was no rational relation between the failure to work and the charge of fraud.

Despite the broad language of the Thirteenth Amendment, the Supreme Court in 1866 upheld an act of Congress which punished seamen who broke their shipping articles. The decision rested on historical grounds. Sailors had always been treated differently from ordinary employees because of conditions on board ships. Later, however, Congress removed this anachronism from the law.

There are, however, conditions under which a state may obtain forced labor from its citizens and punish them if they fail to perform it. Road building, jury duty, militia service are among the duties which the state may exact. In addition, convicts may be compelled to perform labor while in confinement, such labor being expressly excepted from the scope of the amendment.

During wartime, workers have been prevented from freely moving from job to job. No constitutional test of these restrictions has been attempted; in all probability, no such test would succeed. Compulsory service by civilians in time of war has never been attempted in the United States, though it was several times proposed during World War II. There would seem to be little ground for constitutional attack on such service if performed for the state; questions would probably arise only if private employers received some benefit from the forced labor.

6. Rights in Wartime and Military Service

War and fear of war have led to many interferences with liberty. The first occasion arose under the Alien and Sedition Laws of 1798 (see p. 21). The second was during the Civil War when the military authorities, with the approval of President Lincoln, persistently ignored civil rights. They also ignored court writs, but, as Chief Justice Taney regretfully noted, the courts were able to do no more than protest. But after the war was won the Supreme Court invalidated convictions of civilians by military commissions which sat in parts of the country not involved in actual warfare. Justice Davis said (4 Wall. 2, 1866):

> Those great and good men [namely the authors of the Constitution] foresaw that troublous times would arise, when rulers and people would become restive under restraint, and seek by sharp and decisive measures to accomplish ends deemed just and proper; and that the principles of constitutional liberty would be in peril, unless established by irrepealable law. The history of the world had taught them that what was done in the past might be attempted in the future. The Constitution of the United States is a law for rulers and people, equally in war and in peace, and covers with the shield of its protection all classes of men, at all times, and under all circumstances. No doctrine, involving more pernicious consequences, was ever invented by the wit of man than that any of its provisions can be suspended during any of the great exigencies of government.

During World War I, as we have seen (see section 1a) there were many prosecutions under the Espionage Act, especially of leaders of the Socialist party for speeches in opposition to the war and to recruiting. In a case where twenty-year sentences had been imposed on a small group of persons for distributing pamphlets condemning American intervention in the civil war going on in Russia, threatening the newly formed Soviet Government, Justice Holmes wrote an eloquent dissent. He said (250 U.S. 616, 1919):

Persecution for the expression of opinions seems to me perfectly logical. If you have no doubt of your premises or your power and want a certain result with all your heart you naturally express your wishes in law and sweep away all opposition. To allow opposition by speech seems to indicate that you think the speech impotent, as when a man says that he has squared the circle, or that you do not care whole-heartedly for the result, or that you doubt either your power or your premises. But when men have realized that time has upset many fighting faiths, they may come to believe even more than they believe the very foundations of their own conduct that the ultimate good desired is better reached by free trade in ideas—that the best test of truth is the power of the thought to get itself accepted in the competition of the market, and that truth is the only ground upon which their wishes safely can be carried out. That at any rate is the theory of our Constitution. It is an experiment, as all life is an experiment. Every year if not every day we have to wager our salvation upon some prophecy based upon imperfect knowledge. While that experiment is part of our system I think that we should be eternally vigilant against attempts to check the expression of opinions that we loathe and believe to be fraught with death, unless they so imminently threaten immediate interference with the lawful and pressing purposes of the law that an immediate check is required to save the country.

No comparable prosecutions occurred during World War II or the hostilities in Korea and Vietnam.

The draft, with its problem of conscientious objectors, has

produced a vast amount of litigation, especially since the war in Vietnam. Attendant civilians as well as soldiers have had to contend with military trials. Soldiers have been concerned about the kind of discharge they get. Wars bring treason trials. World War II brought the wholesale evacuation of persons of Japanese descent from the West Coast. Finally, the use of state troops in civil disorders has presented legal problems.

6a. *Draftees*

A draftee can challenge his induction, but only on the ground that some legal or constitutional right has been violated.

The rights of draftees have been well described in various publications and need not be detailed here. Important, however, is the method by which a draftee can challenge his classification as 1-A. For a long time it was supposed that a draftee had only two alternatives: to refuse to submit to induction and run the risk of criminal prosecution; or to be inducted and hope that a court would accept his contention when raised in a habeas corpus proceeding. But in 1968 the Court ruled that a suit could be brought in federal court to challenge a classification and to enjoin an order to appear for induction when the draft board had canceled a deferment given to a divinity student. The decision rested on the fact that this exemption had been expressly given by Congress, that there was no dispute about the man's status and that his exemption had been revoked only because he had turned in his draft card in protest against the war in Vietnam.

The principle of that case was extended to cover all kinds of punitive reclassifications where the draftee had been deferred under applicable regulations of the Selective Service System. But the Court refused to apply that rule to the case

of a man who claimed that he had been improperly denied
classification as a conscientious objector. There, the Court
noted there was a factual issue that could not be decided in a
suit to enjoin induction.

The law makes it a crime to fail to register for the draft.
The government prosecuted a man long after the period of
five years during which he could have been prosecuted for his
original failure, claiming that the offense was a continuing
one so that the statute of limitations had no application. The
Supreme Court rejected that contention.

6b. *Pacifists*

Many years ago the Supreme Court ruled that citizenship
could be denied to pacifists on the ground that the law required applicants for citizenship to agree to bear arms. In
1946 those rulings were expressly overruled. And in 1950 the
Court made it clear that applicants for citizenship now need
not agree to perform any military service whatever, whether
combatant or noncombatant.

But the status of pacifists is without constitutional protection. They can be drafted into the army, the exemption
granted to conscientious objectors being only by grace of
Congress. Pacifist students who refuse to attend a course in
military training can be expelled from state universities. The
Supreme Court upheld a denial by Illinois of the right to practice law only because the applicant was a pacifist. The state
court had based its action on a requirement of the Illinois
Constitution, which lawyers had to swear to support, that all
male adults must perform military service in time of war.

The problems of conscientious objectors have troubled the
courts for a long time. While such objector has no constitutional protection, the Supreme Court years ago ruled that a
local draft board's refusal to classify a person as a conscien-

tious objector could be challenged if the decision lacked support in the record. Then the question arose whether the test laid down by Congress had been met by the particular registrant. Congress has exempted those persons who by "religious training and belief" are opposed to participation in war in any form. The test is further defined as being a "belief in a relation to a Supreme Being involving duties superior to those arising from any human relation."

In the *Seeger* case, decided in 1965, the Supreme Court ruled that this definition did not require belief in God. The claims of three persons were involved. Seeger had been unwilling to admit or deny belief in a Supreme Being. He said he believed in devotion to virtue and goodness for their own sakes and that he had a purely ethical creed. One of the other men, Jakobson, did state belief in a Supreme Being as creator. The third man, Peter, hedged the question about a Supreme Being and accepted a definition of religion as belief in "some power manifest in nature which helps man in the ordering of his life in harmony with its demands." The Supreme Court ruled that all three were entitled to classification as conscientious objectors. Justice Clark said (380 U.S. 163):

> The examiner is furnished a standard that permits consideration of criteria with which he has had considerable experience. While the applicant's words may differ, the test is simple of application. It is essentially an objective one, namely, does the claimed belief occupy the same place in the life of the objector as an orthodox belief in God holds in the life of one clearly qualified for exemption?
>
> Moreover, it must be remembered that in resolving these exemption problems one deals with the beliefs of different individuals who will articulate them in a multitude of ways. In such an intensely personal area, of course, the claim of the registrant that his belief is an essential part of a religious faith must be given great weight.

In 1970 the rule of that case was extended to cover a man who stated his belief that all war was immoral, although he had denied that his views were based on religion.

In 1971 the Supreme Court ruled, with only Justice Douglas dissenting, that the exemption from the draft granted to conscientious objectors did not cover those who objected only to a particular war, such as that in Viet Nam. The objection had to be to all war.

The Court upheld a regulation which prohibited a draftee from asking his draft board to consider a claim of conscientious objection made for the first time after the board had sent out an induction notice. In such a case the draftee must make his claim to the military authorities after induction. Justices Douglas, Brennan, and Marshall dissented.

6c. *Military Trials*

During World War II the Supreme Court upheld the right of a military tribunal to sentence to death German saboteurs who were landed on our shores from a submarine. Later the Court ruled that military courts could not try civilians in Hawaii despite the establishment of martial law there. Numerous unsuccessful attempts were made by both German and Japanese soldiers condemned as war criminals to get the Supreme Court to review their convictions. Those tried by military commissions set up by an American general were able to have their convictions reviewed on the merits by the Supreme Court, but failed to have them set aside. Those convicted by tribunals set up by the Allied powers could not get review at all, since the Supreme Court declared it was without jurisdiction to pass on the acts of an international tribunal.

During the American occupation of Germany many persons were convicted of various offenses by military tribunals. The Supreme Court ruled that no American court had jurisdiction to review the convictions of German nationals. In dealing with convictions of American nationals the Court pursued a

curious course for a number of years, making distinctions between cases involving dependents of soldiers and those of civilians, and also whether capital punishment was involved.
Finally, in 1960 the Court ruled against any military trials of
civilians, including dependents of soldiers.

Even a soldier cannot be tried by court-martial for offenses
committed outside a military reservation in the United States
in peacetime when the offense was unrelated to his military
duties. Nor can a discharged soldier be tried by court-martial
even for an offense committed while in the service if it was
not discovered until after his discharge.

In 1971 the Court unanimously upheld a court-martial conviction of a soldier for a crime committed against a civilian on
a military base on the ground that the place at which the
crime was committed made it a service-related matter.

The extent to which a soldier can review a court-martial
conviction in the ordinary courts remains unclear. In a case in
which the convicted men claimed that they had been denied
due process because confessions had been improperly obtained and favorable evidence suppressed by the military, the
justices of the Supreme Court so differed among themselves
that no one can be sure how such a case would be decided if it
came up again. An attempt to review a dishonorable discharge following a court-martial by suit in the Court of
Claims to recover lost pay failed on the ground that the challenge to the court-martial proceedings did not rest on a constitutional basis.

6d. *Discharges*

When the army refused a soldier an honorable discharge
because of his conduct before he had become a soldier he sued
to compel the grant of the honorable discharge. The Supreme
Court decided in his favor on the ground that the army was
without power to consider preinduction conduct.

6e. *Treason*

Treason is narrowly defined in Article III of the Constitution as follows:

> Section 3. Treason against the United States, shall consist only in levying War against them, or in adhering to their Enemies, giving them Aid and Comfort. No Person shall be convicted of Treason unless on the Testimony of two Witnesses to the same overt Act, or on Confession in open Court.
>
> The Congress shall have Power to declare the Punishment of Treason, but no Attainder of Treason shall work Corruption of Blood, or Forfeiture except during the Life of the Person attainted.

Here is another instance of the desire of the Founders to make it impossible for a government to accuse a person of treason on vague grounds. The Supreme Court has dealt with this provision in only two situations. The first, in 1807, involved the conspiracy which led to the trial and acquittal of Aaron Burr, who had been Jefferson's first Vice-President. Two of his alleged confederates challenged the right of a court in the District of Columbia to try them. Chief Justice Marshall ruled that they could not be tried there as none of the acts charged had been committed there. He went on to say that mere conspiracy to overthrow the government without the actual assembling of persons to carry it out could not be treason.

The second group of cases grew out of World War II. In one of these the Court, by a 5 to 4 vote, reversed a conviction on the ground that the charge that the accused man had in fact given aid and comfort to the enemy had not been established by the two witnesses required by the Constitution. In the second case a naturalized citizen of German origin was convicted on the charge that he had harbored his son, one of the saboteurs landed by submarine, knowing that he was a spy for Nazi Germany, and that he had helped him buy an automobile to be used in his spying activities. The problem, as in the earlier case, was whether the crucial matters had been testified to by the required two witnesses. This time the Supreme Court, with only one dissent, upheld the conviction. Justice Douglas could see no real difference between the two cases. A third case involved a native-born man of Japanese ancestry who went to Japan before the war with that country and while there attempted to renounce his American citizenship. He was charged with brutality toward American prisoners of war. After Japan's surrender he again claimed American citizenship. The judge told the jury that they must decide whether the man had intended to renounce American citizenship when in Japan. The Supreme Court upheld the conviction of treason on the ground that this was a question for the jury and that the evidence was sufficient for them to find that the defendant had not renounced his American citizenship.

The last clause of Article III, Section 3, dealing with forfeitures, was considered by the Supreme Court in a Civil War case. Congress had passed a law which purported to confiscate property of those who had rebelled. As it was applied to reach only a life estate of a rebel and not the property itself the Supreme Court ruled that this was an exercise of the war power, not an implementation of the treason section.

Whether an alien residing here can be found guilty of treason has not been explicitly decided, although there are statements in opinions of the Court looking both ways.

6f. *Citizens and Aliens of "Enemy" Descent*

After the shock of the attack on Pearl Harbor fear was expressed on the West Coast that the Japanese might attack there and that many of the residents of Japanese ancestry might help any invaders or commit acts of sabotage. The gen-

eral commanding the troops in the area asked for and obtained authority to impose a curfew in the area on all Japanese and persons of Japanese ancestry. Later they were
ordered to register and assemble in camps. Thousands were
detained during the war. A few resisted and were prosecuted
for violation of the regulations.

Three cases reached the Supreme Court. In the first the
curfew requirement was upheld as incident to the war power.
Chief Justice Stone said (320 U.S. 81, 1943) that the power to
wage war was "the power to wage war successfully" and that
the curfew "was a protective measure necessary to meet the
threat of sabotage and espionage." He justified the singling
out of persons of Japanese ancestry because "residents having ethnic affiliations with an invading enemy may be a
greater source of danger than those of different ancestry."
Justice Murphy expressed the view that the case went "to the
very brink of constitutional power." But when the right to
detain these persons in camps came before the Court it used
the earlier case as binding precedent. This time there were
three dissents, from Justices Roberts, Jackson, and Murphy.
However, at the same time the Court decided that there was
no justification for any longer keeping a person in detention
about whose loyalty to the United States there had been no
question whatever. Ultimately all were released and steps
were taken to compensate them for loss of property. Most
students of the subject consider the detention of citizens of
Japanese ancestry one of the worst blots on the history of the
United States. It has often been remarked that if Justices
Black and Douglas had joined the dissenters in the second of
these cases the detention program would have been condemned.

6g. *Use of Troops in Civil Disturbances*

The federal courts are reluctant to pass on the propriety of
military action taken by a state to control civil disturbance.

In 1909 the Supreme Court refused to interfere with a state's detention of labor leaders after martial law had been declared because disorders were anticipated in connection with a labor dispute. But when a governor of Texas declared a state of martial law so that he could enforce a certain method of oil production the Supreme Court upheld an injunction granted by a lower federal court on the ground that the declaration of martial law was arbitrary under the existing circumstances.

During the disturbance which attended the integration of public schools pursuant to a federal court order in Little Rock, Arkansas, Governor Faubus called out the National Guard to stop the integration on the plea that this move was necessary to preserve the peace. The federal court ruled that this was improper; the Court of Appeals affirmed this ruling and the Supreme Court refused to review it.

7. The Right to Bear Arms

Your right to carry arms can be regulated in the interest of public safety.

The problem of the use of arms by the civilian population was prominent in the minds of the men who drafted the Bill of Rights. Theirs was still a frontier civilization, with the Indian remaining a menace. The people looked to the local militia as protection against enemies abroad and despots at home. So two provisions were included in the Bill of Rights. The Second Amendment declared that the right of the people to bear arms "shall not be infringed." The Third Amendment prohibited the quartering of soldiers in the homes of the people altogether in time of peace and permitted it in time of war only as fixed by law.

These provisions have seldom been invoked. Indeed the Third Amendment can be considered as obsolete. The Second has not been considered a ban on regulation. Various laws restricting the carrying of certain kinds of arms have been upheld on the theory that government had a right to take steps to lessen criminal activities. The assassinations of President Kennedy, of Martin Luther King, and of Senator Robert Kennedy spurred demands for more stringent laws dealing with the acquisition of firearms. These have been opposed by various interested organizations, including hunters, with the result that only rather mild legislation has been enacted.

8. The Right to Travel

You can travel anywhere in the United States.
Your travel outside the United States can be restricted.

The right to move freely from one state to another is one of the few rights which the Supreme Court has declared to be derived from national citizenship and, therefore, protected by the "privileges and immunities" clauses of the original Constitution and of the Fourteenth Amendment. These clauses, by their terms, benefit only citizens. Moreover the protection afforded is only against state action, not action by individuals. In 1920 the Court ruled that Congress had no power to punish persons who forcibly removed a citizen from his home state and threatened him with injury if he returned.

A few years later the Court rebuffed Mayor Hague of Jersey City when he ordered his police to remove protesters whose presence in his city he did not like. The CIO and the American Civil Liberties Union, who were prevented from holding meetings, sued in federal court to enjoin the practice. The Supreme Court decided in favor of the CIO but against the ACLU—the distinction being that the former was an unincorporated association of individuals, whereas the latter was a corporation. As a corporation the ACLU was not covered by the privileges and immunities clause!

In 1969 the Supreme Court ruled that to deprive persons of welfare assistance merely because they had not resided in a state for a year violated their right to move freely throughout the country. Justice Brennan said (394 U.S. 618):

> We do not doubt that the one-year waiting-period device is well suited to discourage the influx of poor families in need of assistance. An indigent who desires to migrate, resettle, find a new job, and start a new life will doubtless hesitate if he knows that he must risk making the move without the possibility of falling back on state welfare assistance during his first year of residence, when his need may be most acute. But the purpose of inhibiting migration by needy persons into the State is constitutionally impermissible.

> This Court long ago recognized that the nature of our Federal Union and our constitutional concepts of personal liberty unite to require that all citizens be free to travel throughout the length and breadth of our land uninhibited by statutes, rules, or regulations which unreasonably burden or restrict this movement.

Many years earlier a California law which punished anyone who brought an indigent person into the state was struck down as in violation of congressional power over interstate commerce, although four of the justices also relied on the privileges and immunities clause. The value of the majority decision is that it benefited aliens as well as citizens.

In 1958 the Court held for the first time that travel outside the country was constitutionally protected so that the State Department could not refuse to issue passports to persons merely because they were suspected of Communist affiliations. Later the Court held unconstitutional a provision of the Internal Security Act which forbade the issuance of passports to members of the Communist party.

The Court, however, ruled that it was permissible for the Secretary of State to refuse passports for travel to Cuba because of the breach in our relations with Castro. But it later held that no law authorized the prosecution of persons who traveled to countries declared out of bounds by the State Department because of conditions prevailing there.

Local authorities have used many devices to keep supposed undesirables away. There are communities in which it is made uncomfortable for Negroes to be around after dark. In some they are not allowed to live unless they are servants in a white person's home. None of these restrictions could stand up if challenged, but too often economic motives lead to acquiescence.

Rights to
Equal Treatment

The equal protection clause protects against discrimination on racial, religious, or political grounds. It covers fields such as schools and transportation, juries, housing, and voting. To some extent it covers sex. Various procedures have been devised to implement its protections. The Bill of Rights contained no provision guaranteeing equal rights to all persons, for the obvious reason that slavery existed. But after the Civil War and the outlawing of slavery by the Thirteenth Amendment, Congress proposed the Fourteenth to insure that there would be no discrimination against the former slaves. This amendment provides that no state shall deny any person the "equal protection of the laws." Congress thought also that another part of that amendment might be useful to the same end: that which guarantees the "privileges and immunities" of citizenship. This second clause, however, has had little significance because the Supreme Court soon ruled that most of the rights for protection of which this provision was invoked, such as the right to vote or freely assemble, were rights derived from state rather than national citizenship.

9. Freedom from Racial Discrimination

While the Fourteenth Amendment does not speak in terms of race it has been most frequently and successfully invoked in aid of the Negroes and other racial groups, such as Mexicans and Chinese, both citizens and aliens. The problems of voting are separately discussed in section 12b.

9a. *Schools and Transportation*

Segregation along racial lines continued in many parts of the country, especially in the South, for nearly a century after the adoption of the Fourteenth Amendment. It was officially approved by the Supreme Court in 1896 in the case of *Plessy* v. *Ferguson*. There the Court upheld a state law which compelled separate railroad accommodations for whites and Negroes but laid down the rule that they must be equal: "separate but equal," the doctrine came to be called. The Court shortly afterward held that a law which forbade furnishing any sleeping accommodations on trains violated this principle.

In 1950 the Court made it plain that there could be no equality in a segregated professional school because of the importance in such an institution of the give and take among the students themselves.

Finally in the famous *Brown* case the Court in 1954 unanimously repudiated the old doctrine of "separate but equal."

That decision affected public schools, but it was soon extended to all public facilities, such as parks, museums, bathing beaches, golf courses, bus lines, and even to admission to athletic events. An attempt to restrict to white persons a park open only to members failed because any white person could become a member. The Court held it improper to expel a member of a residential park open only to white persons because he had leased a house to a Negro.

The statement by Chief Justice Warren in *Brown* is worth quoting at length (347 U.S. 483):

> To separate them [schoolchildren] from others of similar age and qualifications solely because of their race generates a feeling of inferiority as to their status in the community that may affect their hearts and minds in a way unlikely ever to be undone. The effect of this separation on their educational opportunities was well stated by a finding in the Kansas case by a court which nevertheless felt compelled to rule against the negro plaintiffs:
>
>> "Segregation of white and colored children in public schools has a detrimental effect upon the colored children. The impact is greater when it has the sanction of the law; for the policy of separating the races is usually interpreted as denoting the inferiority of the negro group. A sense of inferiority affects the motivation of a child to learn. Segregation with the sanction of law, therefore, has a tendency to retard the educational and mental development of negro children and to deprive them of some of the benefits they would receive in a racially integrated school system."
>
> Whatever may have been the extent of psychological knowledge at the time of *Plessy* v. *Ferguson,* this finding is amply supported by modern authority. Any language in *Plessy* v. *Ferguson* contrary to this finding is rejected.
>
> We conclude that in the field of public education the doctrine of "separate but equal" has no place. Separate educational facilities are inherently unequal.

Unfortunately the Court delayed for a year before it promulgated rules for the implementation of the decision in

Brown. Then it called for desegregation "with all deliberate speed." But opposition in parts of the South had had time to organize. A great variety of laws were passed in attempts to evade or delay integration. After federal troops had to be called in to protect the handful of Negro children who wanted to go to the predominantly white schools in Little Rock, Arkansas, the Court in a special session called in the late summer of 1958 emphasized the supremacy of federal law and condemned "evasive schemes for segregation whether attempted 'ingeniously or ingenuously'."

Still the actual process of desegregation has been painfully slow. Finally, in 1964, the Court insisted that there be immediate desegregation. Under authority of the Civil Rights Act the federal government has sued several states to get speedy results. Resistance to integration has not been limited to the South.

The Court, in 1968, set aside various plans that would have given parents "freedom-of-choice" of schools or permitted them to ask to have their children transferred.

In April 1971 Chief Justice Burger handed down four opinions for a unanimous Court in which he reiterated earlier declarations that state-imposed segregation in schools must be eliminated "root and branch." In the principal opinion he upheld a lower federal court's order that school children can be bused as a means of desegregation. While rejecting the notion that every school in an area must reflect the racial composition of the whole system, the Court approved the use of a mathematical ratio in Charlotte-Mecklenburg County, North Carolina, because the school board had consistently refused to submit any desegregation plan of its own. The Court also noted that pairing of schools might be proper even though they were not contiguous. In another case the Court declared unconstitutional North Carolina's law that forbade "involuntary" busing or the assignment of students for the purpose of creating racial balance. The Court also approved a lower federal court order that assigned teachers so as to accomplish

faculty desegregation. It reversed a decision by the Supreme
Court of Georgia which had, at the behest of white parents,
set aside racial assignments made by a school board.

The Chief Justice said (402 U.S. 1):

> Absent a constitutional violation there would be no basis for
> judicially ordering assignment of students on a racial basis. All
> things being equal, with no history of discrimination, it might
> well be desirable to assign pupils to schools nearest their homes.
>
> But all things are not equal in a system that has been deliber-
> ately constructed and maintained to enforce racial segregation.
> The remedy for such segregation may be administratively awk-
> ward, inconvenient and even bizarre in some situations and may
> impose burdens on some; but all awkwardness and inconven-
> ience cannot be avoided in the interim period when remedial ad-
> justments are being made to eliminate the dual school systems.
>
> No fixed or even substantially fixed guidelines can be estab-
> lished as to how far a court can go, but it must be recognized
> that there are limits. The objective is to dismantle the dual
> school system.

The effect of these decisions is to vest broad discretion in
the lower federal courts to deal with changes that may result.
In that connection Chief Justice Burger said:

> At some point, these school authorities and others like them
> should have achieved full compliance with this Court's decision
> in Brown. The systems will then be "unitary" in the sense re-
> quired by our decisions in Green and Alexander.
>
> It does not follow that the communities served by such sys-
> tems will remain demographically stable, for in a growing, mo-
> bile society, few will do so. Neither school authorities nor dis-
> trict courts are constitutionally required to make year-by-year
> adjustments of the racial composition of student bodies once the
> affirmative duty to desegregate has been accomplished and ra-
> cial discrimination through official action is elminated from the
> system.

This does not mean that Federal courts are without power to deal with future problems; but in the absence of a showing that either the school authorities or some other agency of the state has deliberately attempted to fix or alter demographic patterns to affect the racial composition of the schools, further intervention by a district court should not be necessary.

In June 1973 in a case involving the Denver school system, the Court found that although segregation had not been established by law, it did in fact exist in much of the system. It remanded the case to give the school board time to prove that neighborhood schools had been segregated unintentionally. Justice Rehnquist dissented; Justices Powell and Douglas asked the Court to outlaw all de facto segregation.

An interesting method of enforcing school integration was developed in a suit brought in a federal court in Mississippi by Negro taxpayers and their minor school-attending children. The suit sought to prevent the Internal Revenue Service from granting exemption from income taxes to schools that discriminated against Negroes and from allowing tax deductibility for their contributions. A three-judge "statutory" court ruled that the schools would not be able to function without tax deductible contributions and granted a preliminary injunction pending a trial to determine whether, in fact, the schools were unconstitutionally segregated.

9b. *Jury Service*

Almost immediately after the Civil War many states in the South passed laws aimed at keeping Negroes from serving on juries. The Supreme Court at once struck these down as violating the Fourteenth Amendment. Nevertheless, Negroes were kept off juries by various discriminatory devices. In a number of cases in which the state authorities made no attempt to deny these practices, convictions of Negroes were reversed by the Supreme Court on the ground that discrimination against Negroes in the selection of either the grand jury that indicted them or the jury that tried them violated the guarantee of equal protection. But the Court made it plain that no one could complain merely because no person of his own race had sat on one of these juries.

Until the Scottsboro case arose in the 1930s there had been no real attempt by lawyers for convicted Negroes to prove that there had been discrimination when this was denied by the state authorities. The Scottsboro case involved a charge of rape against nine young Negroes. The first convictions were set aside by the Supreme Court because the defendants had not received effective assistance of lawyers (see section 34b). When the second round of trials commenced, a well-known New York criminal lawyer, Samuel S. Leibowitz (later a judge), was retained. He called many Negroes from the communities where the grand jury had sat and where the trials were taking place and established that although qualified to be jurors they had never been called for service and that no Negro had been called for many years. The state officials denied any intention to discriminate. Although their denials were accepted by the state courts, the United States Supreme Court looked into the facts for itself and concluded that there had been intentional discrimination.

Discrimination in the selection of the grand jury that indicted will result in reversal of a conviction even though there was no discrimination in the selection of the trial jury. In one case the Supreme Court, even though there were a few Negroes on the list, found discrimination on the ground that fair selection would have resulted in many more Negroes being on the list. As Justice Black said: "If there has been discrimination, whether accomplished ingeniously or ingenuously, the conviction cannot stand." On the other hand, a rape conviction of a Negro was sustained even though the prosecution had succeeded in eliminating all the Negroes who had

been called up. The majority of the Court concluded that this
was not being done systematically.

The question of women jurors is separately discussed (see
section 33a).

9c. *Sex Relations*

You can enter into a biracial marriage.

Many states have laws prohibiting interracial marriages
and providing more severe punishment for adultery where
the parties are of different races than when they are both of
the same race. The Supreme Court upheld a law of the latter
category in 1883 on the theory that the same punishment was
imposed on both the white and the Negro adulterers. The
Court did not deal with the marriage prohibition until 1967.
Then it unanimously struck down a Virginia law which
barred interracial marriages. A few years earlier it had held
invalid a Florida law which punished unmarried persons of
different race and sex for occupying the same room.

9d. *Housing*

*You can buy or rent a house even if the property is subject to
a covenant which excludes persons of your race.*

In many parts of the country racial discrimination in housing was accomplished by private agreements not to sell or
rent to a nonwhite person; the agreements sometimes excluded Jews as well as Negroes. It was for a long time taken
for granted that such agreements could not be challenged
under the Fourteenth Amendment since they were not made
under any state law and that amendment restricted state action only. But in 1948 the Supreme Court ruled that such

agreements could not be enforced by injunctions since enforcement required action by the courts, which were agencies of the states. After state courts had differed as to whether suits at law for damages could be maintained for ignoring such covenants, the Supreme Court in 1953 decided that issue in the negative.

Many years ago the Supreme Court had upheld West Coast legislation which barred Japanese aliens from holding land. A later attempt to enforce the law was frustrated, but only because the Supreme Court struck down a presumption which operated against American-born sons of these aliens. In another case the Court held a state law unconstitutional because it was discriminatory in seeking to deprive Japanese aliens of fishing rights, pointing out that the state's power over fishing was not as great as its power over real estate.

In 1967 the Court upheld a California decision that a newly adopted constitutional provision which forbade legislation restricting discrimination in housing constituted state action in aid of discrimination and, therefore, violated the equal protection clause. In another case the Court held that the equal protection clause was also violated by a city charter provision which abrogated an existing ordinance forbidding discrimination in housing unless it was approved by a majority of the electors, because the "gauntlets" so established dealt only with housing discrimination and placed a burden on racial minorities.

But a few years later the Court upheld a state law which provided that before a low-rent housing project could be erected in any community the voters had to approve it. Justice Black said that the law was not racially motivated and that the "thrust" of the equal protection clause was to outlaw discrimination on account of race. He noted, moreover, that the procedure was democratic because it gave the people of a community the right to pass on matters which might affect the taxes they would have to pay and the future development

111

of their community. Justice Marshall, in dissent, insisted the law was discriminatory against the poor and that it was "far too late in the day" to limit the equal protection clause to racial discrimination. He was joined by Justices Brennan and Blackmun—this being the latter's first important disagreement with the Chief Justice. Justice Douglas abstained.

In June 1968 the Court made a far-reaching decision in *Jones* v. *Mayer* by upholding a law passed in 1866 implementing the Thirteenth Amendment. This law declared, among other things, that all citizens, regardless of color, had the right to buy and rent land. This, said the majority, authorized an injunction against a private person to bar discrimination. Justice Stewart said (392 U.S. 409):

> As its text reveals, the Thirteenth Amendment "is not a mere prohibition of state laws establishing or upholding slavery, but an absolute declaration that slavery or involuntary servitude shall not exist in any part of the United States." [*Civil Rights cases*, 109 U.S. 3, 20.] It has never been doubted, therefore, "that the power vested in Congress to enforce the article by appropriate legislation" [ibid.] includes the power to enact laws "direct and primary, operating upon the acts of individuals, whether sanctioned by state legislation or not." [Id. at 23.]
>
> Thus the fact that Section 1982 operates upon the unofficial acts of private individuals, whether or not sanctioned by state law, presents no constitutional problem. If Congress has power under the Thirteenth Amendment to eradicate conditions that prevent Negroes from buying and renting property because of their race or color, then no federal statute calculated to achieve that objective can be thought to exceed the constitutional power of Congress simply because it reaches beyond state action to regulate the conduct of private individuals.

In 1971 the Court let stand a ruling that the City of Lackawanna, New York, had promoted racial segregation by refusing to allow the construction of low-income housing in a white neighborhood.

9e. *Miscellaneous*

The Court unanimously reversed convictions for contempt of Negroes who refused to obey a judge's order to withdraw from a part of the courtroom reserved for whites and a contempt conviction of a Negro who refused to answer a question because she had been addressed by her first name.

By will a tract of land was left to a city for use as a park for white persons only. After the city allowed Negroes to use it, a state court removed the city as trustee. The Supreme Court reversed this decision, holding that the purpose of that action was to enforce the segregated character of the gift.

The Court unanimously reversed convictions of Negroes for playing basketball in a park on the ground that if these rested on race, it was a denial of equal protection, and if not, defendants had not been advised why they should not play.

The Court has condemned a Louisiana statute requiring designation of the race of each candidate on the ballot as this was but "superficial" equality. The Court later upheld a lower-court decision that held unconstitutional Alabama laws which compelled racial segregation in jails.

A federal appeals court in January 1971 ordered a Mississippi town to stop discriminating against areas occupied by Negroes in services such as paving, sewers, and traffic lights.

In 1964 Congress forbade racial discrimination in employment in industries in interstate commerce. The Supreme Court, in interpreting this law, decided that it was not necessary for a person claiming its benefits to show an intention on the part of the accused employer to discriminate; it was enough to show that the standards set up for employment or promotion were such that discrimination was the likely result, and that these standards were not related to job performance. This decision was made in 1971 in a case challenging a regulation of the Duke Power Company that allegedly restricted Negroes to low-paying jobs unless they were able to

pass two intelligence tests or obtain a high school diploma.
Chief Justice Burger said that the law "proscribes not only
overt discrimination but also practices that are fair in form,
but discriminatory in operation."

But in 1971, by a 5-4 vote, the Court upheld the right of
Jackson, Mississippi, to close all public swimming pools to
avoid a federal court order to integrate them.

10. Freedom from Nonracial Discrimination

Discrimination has been practiced at various times and places
on grounds other than race. Religious and political minorities,
homosexuals, women, have all suffered from restrictions on
their activities and their employment. The Supreme Court
has generally struck down discriminatory laws and government practices unless it concluded they had a reasonable
basis.

10a. *Sex*

The most pervasive and persistent discrimination has involved women. The slogan that this is a man's world has been
all too true. Until about a century ago married women had no
rights over their own property. Women were unable to vote
in most parts of the United States until 1920. While they had
opened the doors to higher education and most of the professions well before 1920, it was not until almost yesterday that
they broke the masculine exclusiveness of colleges such as
Harvard, Yale, and Princeton. Women have become judges,
but hardly ever of appellate courts. No woman has ever sat
on the Supreme Court of the United States. Today women
play in all the important musical ensembles but no great or-
chestra has a woman conductor. There have been only occasional women Cabinet ministers, United States senators,

members of the House of Representatives, or governors. And women do not receive the same pay as men for the same work in many occupations.

There are also still some discriminations against women in the operation of the law. Some communities punish certain offenses more severely if committed by a woman; some women's prisons are inferior to those in which men are confined. It is notorious, moreover, that when a house of prostitution is raided the female inmates are prosecuted, the male patrons let go.

Discrimination in employment has been rampant, although somewhat on the wane since the enactment of the Civil Rights Act of 1964 which forbids such discrimination by reason of sex by employers engaged in interstate commerce. That law has had some curious results. A man who wanted to become an airline steward won on appeal because the court found that the preference for women stewardesses was not necessary for the successful operation of the airline. In some cases the new law appears to conflict with state laws aimed at the protection of women. So a court held that a law barring women from certain kinds of heavy work could be sustained only if it could be established that there were no women capable of doing that work without injury to themselves, a requirement impossible to comply with.

In January 1971 the Supreme Court dealt with sex discrimination under the 1964 law. A mother of seven children was rejected as an assembly-line trainee on the ground that the company had a rule against hiring mothers of young children. The lower federal courts ruled that the exclusion was not barred by the law because it rested, not on the fact of sex, but on the fact of motherhood. The Supreme Court unanimously disagreed, noting that fathers of young children were not barred by the company. The Court sent the case back for a hearing to determine whether parenthood was "more relevant to job performance for a woman than for a man."

An amusing incident occurred in New York City in the summer of 1970. For some time a few women had tried to get into a bar that was notoriously limited to men, McSorley's Old Ale House in the East Village. One of them brought a law suit to compel their admission. A lower federal court decided in their favor on the ground that the state of New York, through its supervisory power over places that sold liquor, had participated in discrimination against them. Shortly afterward Mayor Lindsay signed a city ordinance that banned discrimination on account of sex at places of public entertainment. So on the afternoon of the signing several women went to the bar and were admitted after some futile skirmishing. The bartender asked one of them to produce a birth certificate to show she was over the age of eighteen, below which it is illegal to serve a person liquor.

It is small wonder, therefore, that a "Women's Liberation" movement has arisen, although many of its advocates and objectives may make little sense, and that a constitutional amendment has been proposed to establish equal rights for women. One may well ask why such an amendment may be needed in the light of the requirement of the Fourteenth Amendment that no state may deny any person the equal protection of the laws. A partial answer is that the Supreme Court has never interpreted that amendment to require exact equality. It has permitted deviations whenever it found some rational basis for them.

In 1948 the Court upheld a Michigan law which forbade any woman from acting as a barmaid unless she was the wife or daughter of the owner. In 1961 it found no violation of the right to equal protection in a law that let women sit on juries only if they elected to do so, a law that exists in many states. Indeed, there is an intimation in the opinion that a state could deny all women the right to be jurors. The arguments advanced to support this position were that the various laws took into consideration the supposed greater physical weak-

nesses of women, as well as the problems incident to
pregnancy and the care of young children.

In 1971 the Court, for the first time, held a state law
unconstitutional because it discriminated against women.
This was an Idaho statute which gave men preference in
obtaining administration of estates of persons who died
without wills. That, said a unanimous Court, was an arbitrary
distinction.

10b. *Indigents*

The Supreme Court has been concerned over a long period
of time with the rights of the poor. Many years ago it ruled
that a state must furnish a person convicted of crime with a
transcript of the record needed for an appeal if he is too poor
to pay for it, and must let him file his papers without the
payment of the fees required of persons able to pay for them.
Transcripts must be provided even if the offenses are misdemeanors or punishable only by fines, and indigents cannot be
required to pay for them with money they earn in jail if
indigents not in jail are not obliged to repay the cost.

The famous *Gideon* case of 1963 led to the requirement that
states must provide lawyers to indigents charged with crime.
In March 1971 the Court unanimously outlawed the practice
of sending people to jail who are unable to pay the fines
usually imposed for minor offenses. The Court suggested that
some method be worked out for paying such fines in install-
ments. On the same day the Court ruled that it was a denial
of equal protection to require an indigent person to pay fees
in order to begin a suit for divorce. But it is not a denial to
require a fee for bankruptcy proceedings.

The spirit of these cases was not followed a short time later
when the Court, 5-3, upheld a law requiring voter approval
before a low-rent housing project could be built (see section
9d).

10c. *Miscellaneous*

Under Louisiana law recovery is allowed to certain classes of persons for damages resulting from the wrongful death of specified relatives. Among those who can sue are children for the loss of a parent and parents for the loss of a child. Lower courts held that this law did not allow illegitimate children to sue for the death of their mother, nor the mother of an illegitimate child to sue for his death. The Supreme Court reversed both decisions on the ground that this law denied equal protection to illegitimate children.

But in 1971 the Court, in a 5-4 decision, ruled that Louisiana could deny intestate inheritance rights to illegitimate children, largely on the ground that their rights could have been protected had their parent made a will. Justices Douglas, Brennan, White, and Marshall dissented.

In 1969 the Court decided that the equal protection clause was violated by a state denial of welfare assistance to persons who had not resided within the state for at least a year.

Discrimination on religious or political grounds is likewise forbidden. Thus the Court held that it was a denial of equal protection to refuse a permit for a park meeting to the Jehovah's Witnesses when permits had been issued to other religious organizations. But the Court in 1955 refused to pass on a refusal of the Yonkers school board to permit a peace group to use a school auditorium for lack of allegation that the auditorium had been used by similar groups.

In 1972 the Court struck down a Massachusetts law which prohibited distribution of birth control material to unmarried persons, on the ground the state had no adequate reason for discriminating against such persons.

There have been rumblings over what can be called "class" discrimination. These have arisen in suburban communities where zoning regulations prevent building developments that might bring in people less prosperous than those already there. Another grievance is the exaction of high fees for the use of beaches and parks by nonresidents, or even the complete prohibition of access by outsiders.

The Supreme Court's first decision in the area of class discrimination was unfavorable. Five of the Justices upheld a state law which permitted voters in a community to bar low income housing on the ground that they had a right to decide what was suitable for their community so long as there was no discrimination on the ground of race (see section 9d).

In March 1973 the Court held that the right to equal protection is not denied by the prevalent practice of providing school funds out of real estate taxes, even though this results in rich areas being able to spend more money on their schools than poor ones. Justice Powell said that any inequities should be corrected by legislation. Justices Douglas, Brennan, White, and Marshall dissented. Some state courts have held that the practice is barred by the states' own constitutions.

11. Means of Legal Recourse Against Discrimination

Discriminatory laws and practices can be challenged in a variety of ways. Where the discrimination is in the selection of jurors, a conviction for crime will be reversed (see section 9b). In some situations, as with segregation in schools or housing, a law suit can be started to end the practice (see sections 9a and 9d).

From time to time Congress has passed laws to help those who have been discriminated against. In dealing with discriminatory federal agencies its power is almost unlimited, but where the discrimination has been caused by private persons or by state action Congress is restricted to use of the commerce clause or implementation of the equal protection clause of the Fourteenth Amendment. It can prohibit discrimination by private persons only to the extent that interstate or foreign commerce is involved because the Fourteenth Amendment binds state action only. It is important, therefore, to indicate how the Supreme Court has defined state action.

11a. *Interstate Commerce*

Long ago the Supreme Court upheld the right of Congress to forbid discrimination in interstate commerce. It ruled that a railroad regulation which limited dining-car service for Negroes to a particular curtained space was invalid on the ground that the law forbade racial classification of any kind in interstate commerce. The logic of these decisions was applied to a restaurant maintained at an interstate bus terminal.

Doubt whether a state might forbid discrimination in areas affecting interstate commerce was laid at rest in 1963 when a unanimous Court reversed a Colorado decision which prohibited its state Commission against Discrimination from ordering an interstate air carrier to hire a Negro.

And in December 1964 the Court unanimously upheld the "Public Accommodations" section of the 1964 Civil Rights Act on the ground that it rested on the power of Congress to regulate interstate commerce. There were two cases: one involved service to interstate travelers; the other involved a local restaurant where a substantial part of the food served had come from other states.

11b. *Civil Rights Laws*

In 1945 the Supreme Court upheld the constitutionality of the post-Civil War federal Civil Rights Law insofar as it was applied to state officials who had conspired to bring false charges against Negroes and who had beaten them while in jail, but it reversed the conviction on the ground the jury had not been sufficiently instructed that the defendants had not violated the law unless they knew they were infringing rights guaranteed Negroes under the federal Constitution. On a retrial these particular defendants were acquitted. But others have been convicted for like offenses and their convictions sustained by the Supreme Court.

In two civil cases the Court in 1951 narrowed the scope of the federal law designed to prevent interference with civil rights. One case involved the acts of members of a state legislative committee, the other the breaking up of a meeting. The Court ruled that suit could not be brought in either case because the defendants had acted as private individuals only. In June 1971, however, the Court unanimously reversed its position. It held that redress could be obtained in a federal court against private persons who had conspired to deprive Negroes of their rights.

Efforts by the government to enforce the 1957 Civil Rights Law were upheld in two cases.

In 1966 in a case which arose out of the murder in 1964 of three civil rights workers in Mississippi, the Court expressly held that one part of the old civil rights laws included due process rights that were guaranteed against state action by the Fourteenth Amendment as well as those that were guaranteed by the Constitution directly to individuals. The Court also decided that another part reached private persons who participated with state officials in denial of rights "under color of law." The Court also held that interference with the right to travel from state to state was covered by the new law.

But the new law did not touch an ancient doctrine of immunity from suit of certain kinds of public officials. Thus the Court held that a group of clergymen who were convicted of breach of the peace because they attempted to use segregated facilities at an interstate bus terminal could, after reversal, sue the policeman who had made the arrests but not the judge who convicted them. The Court also held that Senator Eastland was immune from a suit based on a claim that he had conspired with state officials to seize a plaintiff's records in violation of the Fourth Amendment, but that counsel to the committee of which Eastland was chairman was not.

The usefulness of these laws was increased in 1968 by a unanimous decision that counsel fees should be awarded a successful plaintiff regardless of a defendant's good faith in defending unless special circumstances would make this unjust.

11c. *State Action*

Since the Fourteenth Amendment bars discrimination only when it is the result of action by a state or its local subdivisions, questions have often arisen with respect to its impact in various areas affecting private activities.

As we have seen (section 9d), enforcement of restrictive covenants was held to constitute state action.

In 1935 the Court approved the refusal of the Democratic party in Texas to allow Negroes to vote in its primaries on the ground that this was private, not state, action. This generally denied Negroes effective participation in elections, for in Texas at that time winning the Democratic primary was almost always equivalent to winning the election. In 1944 the Court overruled that decision and recognized that a state's regulation of primary elections made them part of the state electoral machinery in which discrimination based on race could not be tolerated. Justice Reed said (321 U.S. 649):

> The United States is a constitutional democracy. Its organic law grants to all citizens a right to participate in the choice of elected officials without restriction by any State because of race. This grant to the people of the opportunity for choice is not to

be nullified by a State through casting its electoral process in a form which permits a private organization to practice racial discrimination in the election. Constitutional rights would be of little value if they could be thus indirectly denied.

The decision aroused a storm of denunciation in the South, participated in by members of Congress, governors, and others who proclaimed that "white supremacy" must be preserved. They threatened that the decision would be disregarded or circumvented. South Carolina promptly repealed all of its laws relating to primary elections. The lower federal courts, however, concluded that the repeal of these laws made no difference and that Negroes should be entitled to vote in the Democratic primaries nevertheless. The Supreme Court refused to review their rulings. Another device, that of the "informal" primary, held without use of the state's election machinery, was struck down because the Court believed state action was involved.

In 1960 the Court held that when a privately operated concession was an integral part of an interstate air terminal, discrimination was prohibited by congressional enactment. The Court later ruled that when a state had leased part of a parking garage to a restaurant in order to help finance the operation, that restaurant could not refuse to serve a person because of his race.

In a number of cases involving private establishments the Court was confronted with convictions for disorderly conduct or trespass because of sit-in and freedom ride demonstrations. In 1963 it reversed a number of such convictions because municipal ordinances were referred to by the owner of the establishment and others because the local authorities had stated they would not tolerate integration.

In 1970 the Court sent back for trial a case in which a white woman sued a concern that had refused to serve her when she came with some Negroes on the ground that she claimed there was a state-enforced custom requiring racial discrimination. If that could be established, the Court held, the woman had a right to sue.

In another case the Court held that state action was involved because an amusement park employee who ordered Negroes to leave had arrested them in his capacity as deputy sheriff. The Court also unanimously reversed a decision because it found state involvement through requirements for separate restrooms.

The Court accepted a finding by the California Supreme Court that a constitutional provision barring legislation restricting discrimination in housing constituted state action in aid of discrimination.

In June 1972 the Supreme Court, by a 6-3 vote, reversed a ruling by a lower federal court that a state's supervisory power over places licensed to sell liquor made the state a party to discrimination if it allowed private clubs to refuse service to Negro guests of white members. Justice Rehnquist for the majority said that such supervisory powers did not bring the Fourteenth Amendment into play. Justices Douglas, Brennan, and Marshall dissented. This ruling would undoubtedly be applicable to clubs that are restricted to men or women only (see section 10a).

12. The Right to Vote

In the Constitutional Convention of 1787 a persistent minority sought to have the members of both houses of Congress elected by the state legislature or to limit the suffrage to those who were "freeholders," that is, owners of land. These attempts were ultimately defeated, partly because Benjamin Franklin put his weighty voice in opposition. As finally approved, however, the Constitution left qualifications for voting to the states. In the original Constitution there were also no guarantees whatever against discrimination. The following are the provisions of the Constitution:

The House of Representatives shall be composed of members chosen every second year by the people of the several States, and the electors in each State shall have the qualifications requisite for electors of the most numerous branch of the State Legislature. [Art. I, Sec. 2, cl. 1]

The times, places, and manner of holding elections for Senators and Representatives shall be prescribed in each State by the Legislature thereof; but the Congress may at any time by law make or alter such regulations, except as to the places of choosing Senators. [Art. I, Sec. 4, cl. 1]

Each State shall appoint, in such manner as the Legislature thereof may direct, a number of Electors . . . [Art. II, Sec. 1, cl. 2]

The Congress may determine the time of choosing the Electors, and the day on which they shall give their votes; which day shall be the same throughout the United States. [Art. II, Sec. 1, cl. 4]

The Fourteenth Amendment, in Section 2, contained a provision for reduction of representation in Congress that has never been implemented.

Representatives shall be apportioned among the several States according to their respective numbers, counting the whole number of persons in each State, excluding Indians not taxed. But when the right to vote at any election for the choice of Electors for President and Vice President of the United States, Representatives in Congress, the executive and judicial officers of a State, or the members of the Legislature thereof, is denied to any of the male inhabitants of such State, being twenty-one years of age, and citizens of the United States, or in any way abridged, except for participation in rebellion, or other crime, the basis of representation therein shall be reduced in the proportion which the number of such male citizens shall bear to the whole number of male citizens twenty-one years of age in such State.

Discrimination is forbidden by the Fifteenth and the Nineteenth Amendments. ·

> The right of citizens of the United States to vote shall not be denied or abridged by the United States or by any State on account of race, color, or previous condition of servitude.

The Nineteenth added "sex."

12a. *Eighteen-Year-Olds*

Since June 1971 eighteen-year-olds can vote in local, state, and national elections.

The extent to which Congress can, under the general umbrella of the equal protection clause, modify the only qualifications for voting contained in the Constitution, namely, that they be the same as those of the electors in the largest branch of the state legislature, was tested in 1970 when Congress passed a law giving the vote to eighteen-year-olds. President Nixon when he signed the law expressed doubts about its constitutionality. Several states sued to challenge it.

On the last decision day in 1970 the Supreme Court upheld the law only insofar as it affected national elections. Justice Black joined Justices Douglas, Brennan, White, and Marshall on this phase of the matter. But in declaring that Congress had no power to impose the enfranchisement of eighteen-year-olds in state elections, Justice Black joined Chief Justice Burger and Justices Harlan, Stewart, and Blackmun.

Justice Black rejected the contention that states denied equal protection to persons between eighteen and twenty-one and said (400 U.S. 112):

> It is a plain fact of history that the Framers never imagined that the national Congress would set the qualifications for voters in every election from President to local constable or village

alderman. It is obvious that the whole Constitution reserves to the States the power to set voter qualifications in state and local elections except to the limited extent that the people through constitutional amendments have specifically narrowed the power of the States.

On the other hand he upheld congressional power to lower the voting age in federal elections on the basis of the right given to Congress to regulate these.

The principal dissent with respect to state elections was written by Justice Brennan; that with respect to federal elections by Justice Harlan. The first stressed the various respects in which eighteen-year-olds were given rights by the states and argued that the denial of the right to vote was an unjustifiable discrimination. Justice Harlan stressed the words of the Constitution which fixed the qualifications for persons voting for members of Congress as those provided by the states for their own legislatures.

Congress early in 1971 passed a constitutional amendment giving voting rights to eighteen-year-olds. Ratified in June, it became the Twenty-sixth Amendment.

12b. *Racial Discrimination*

Despite the prohibition against racial discrimination contained in the Fifteenth Amendment the Negro has had a constant struggle to be allowed to register and vote. The Supreme Court has consistently struck down various state laws which attempted to circumvent the amendment. In 1965 Congress passed a Voting Rights Act which has made it possible for Negroes to register and vote in increasing numbers. In the 1970 election a considerable number of Negroes were elected to office even in the deep South.

A brief review of the more significant cases will illustrate the devices that have been used in an attempt to restrict the Negro vote.

Oklahoma passed a law in 1916 which restricted the franchise to persons who had voted in 1914 or had registered between May 10, 1916, and June 30, 1916. In 1939 the Supreme Court held this law unconstitutional because it was plainly designed to eliminate Negroes by the choice of dates. In 1949 the Court upheld a lower-court decision which had voided an Alabama law that granted election officials arbitrary power to disqualify anyone unable to "understand and explain" any article of the state constitution which the official might pick. That decision also rested on the belief that the law had been passed to give officials the right to exclude Negroes. A Louisiana literacy test was struck down because it had been administered in a way that discriminated against Negroes.

At one time the Supreme Court had ruled that primary elections were entirely outside the scope of federal regulation. Later it concluded otherwise, at least in states in which the primary was part of the established election machinery, or where, as was the case in certain southern states, the primary election really determined the outcome of the general election. When Texas eliminated the primary from the election machinery and the Democratic party held an "informal" all-white primary, the Supreme Court ruled this an evasion.

The Supreme Court upheld the provisions of the 1965 Voting Rights Act which sought to correct racial discrimination in connection with registration and voting and which set up machinery for the suspension of state laws found to be discriminatory. In 1969 the Court upheld the suspension of certain literacy tests because a lower court found that the state had given Negroes inferior educational opportunities. The following year the Court unanimously approved an act of Congress which suspended all literacy tests for five years. Earlier the Court had upheld a congressional enactment which declared that any person could vote who had reached a certain level of education. That case resulted in the voiding of New York's requirement that persons desiring to vote take tests in English—a victory for its large Spanish-speaking population.

The 1965 act also prevented states from changing their voting regulations in any way which might diminish the rights of Negroes without the approval of the United States Attorney General or a federal court. Mississippi passed laws which permitted a switch from district to at-large voting for some county supervisors, the appointment of others instead of their election, and restrictions on independent candidates. Virginia's Board of Elections prohibited the use of stickers on ballots by illiterate voters. The Supreme Court held the laws and the regulations to be in violation of the act of Congress but it refused to void elections which had already taken place.

In 1960 the Court upheld a complaint by Negroes that there should be a hearing to decide whether the redistricting of the city of Tuskegee would result in eliminating the Negro vote there. But the Court found no evidence of racial discrimination in the so-called silk-stocking district in New York City. The Court held that Negro candidates had been improperly kept off the ballot in Alabama because white candidates had been put on the ballot although they had not complied with a provision of the law which was used to keep the Negroes off.

12c. *Nonracial Discrimination*

You do not have to pay a poll tax to vote.

Many states, especially in the South, used to require the payment of poll taxes as a condition of voting, usually with the requirement that all back taxes had to be paid up. Thus many poor people were disfranchised. In 1938 the Supreme Court upheld such a requirement. But in 1966 that decision was overruled, the Court declaring that there was no rational relation between the payment of a tax and qualifications for voting. In the meantime the Twenty-fourth Amendment which outlawed the requirement for payment of poll taxes in national elections had been adopted. When Virginia then required that a person who wanted to vote in a national election but had not paid his poll taxes must present a certificate of residence the Supreme Court ruled that this law violated the new amendment. The poll tax would seem to be dead as a qualification for voting.

In 1970 Congress limited residence requirements for voting in federal elections to thirty days. The Supreme Court upheld the law. In 1972 the Court voided a state law which required one year's residence in the state and three months in the county as qualifications for voting in state or local elections. Later it suggested that fifty days was long enough. Earlier the Court had denied Texas the right to prevent a person who had moved into the state while in the military service from voting in any election. Later the Court ruled that no state could deny a person the right to vote because he lived on a federal reservation, such as the National Institutes of Health in Maryland.

12d. *One Man, One Vote*

Ways have been found to deprive many persons of effective participation in the voting machinery, chiefly by inequality in voting districts. Generally the rural areas were favored over the cities. In some states this was accomplished by failing to make changes in the districts to keep up with population changes. In others, such as Georgia, each district was given a single representative in the legislature regardless of its population. The result has been that in many states there were fantastic variations in the population makeups of the districts. In one case the Court noted that there was a discrepancy of up to forty-one to one in the Alabama Senate and up to about sixteen to one in its House. One county with a population of 13,462 had two seats, while another with a population of 314,301 had only three seats.

For many years the Supreme Court had avoided dealing with the problem of improper apportionment on the ground that it was a political, not a justiciable, issue. But in 1962 the Court, in *Baker* v. *Carr,* rejected the old view and laid down the revolutionary principle that there must be an adherence to the "one man, one vote" idea. In accordance with that principle the Court has set aside apportionments in a number of states because of discrepancies in the way districts were set up. The rule now is that there must be substantial equality and that this applies to both houses of a state's legislature. In 1969 the Court voided a Missouri apportionment when the variance was as low as 3.13 percent. This one man, one vote principle has been applied not only to state legislature and congressional districts, but also to local governmental bodies having broad legislative powers. But in a group of decisions handed down in June 1971 the Court permitted certain variations when it was satisfied that they were not intended to discriminate against any particular group in the community.

12e. *Miscellaneous*

The Court upheld a provision in the Georgia Constitution which permitted the legislature to select a governor when no candidate had received a majority of the votes cast at the general election. This 5 to 4 decision ensured the election of Lester G. Maddox as governor.

Complaints by jail inmates that they were deprived of their right to vote while awaiting trial were rejected by the Court.

Restrictions have been common in elections for limited purposes. Thus New York restricted voting in school elections to parents of children attending school and to property owners

or tenants and their spouses, thus disqualifying a bachelor
who lived with his parents. The Supreme Court ruled this to
be a denial of equal protection. It also so ruled with respect to
a Louisiana law which restricted voting on bond issues to taxpayers. These decisions rested on the Court's view that all
generally qualified voters in a community had an interest in
the issues involved.

Restrictions have also been imposed on access to the ballot.
Just before the 1948 election the Court held that Illinois had
the right to require new parties—in this instance the Progressive party—to obtain signatures on its petition from a majority of the state's counties. But in 1969 the Court overruled the
earlier decision and held that such a requirement improperly
discriminated against populous counties in favor of rural
ones. The Court also ruled that Ohio had denied equal protection to the party represented by George Wallace when it
placed severe restrictions on its right to appear on the ballot.
In 1971 the Court upheld a Georgia law which requires petitions signed by five percent of the voters for an independent
candidate to get on the ballot, the Court noting that the law
allowed write-in votes.

A corollary to the citizen's right to vote is the right to be
represented by the candidate he has elected. After the House
of Representatives refused to seat Adam Clayton Powell in
1967 because of misconduct on his part the Supreme Court
held that the House had exceeded its powers. Exclusion, as
opposed to expulsion, was held permissible only if the elected
congressman did not possess the qualifications specified in the
Constitution with respect to age, residence, and citizenship.
Chief Justice Warren said (395 U.S. 486, 1969):

> A fundamental principle of our representative democracy is,
> in Hamilton's words, "that the people should choose whom they
> please to govern them." As Madison pointed out at the Conven-
> tion, this principle is undermined as much by limiting whom the
> people can select as by limiting the franchise itself. In apparent

agreement with this basic philosophy, the Constitution adopted his suggestion limiting the power to expel. To allow essentially that same power to be exercised under the guise of judging qualifications, would be to ignore Madison's warning, borne out in the Wilkes case and some of Congress' own post-Civil War exclusion cases, against "vesting an improper & dangerous power in the Legislature."

In 1972 the Court unanimously struck down a Texas law which imposed large fees on the privilege of running in a primary election. This, said Chief Justice Burger, was an unreasonable burden on the right to be on the ballot. The Court also ruled that state proceedings for a recount in a Senate election did not conflict with the Senate's right to judge the qualifications of its own members.

Miscellaneous Rights

Some rights have been developed that are not explicitly dealt with in the Constitution. Among them are those of citizens, of aliens, and of labor. In recent years the rights of witnesses before investigating committees have assumed great importance. A new right—that to a clean environment—is just beginning to be heard about. Included here are also two provisions from the main body of the Constitution: bills of attainder and ex post facto laws.

13. Rights of Citizens

The citizenship of a native-born American cannot be taken from him except by a voluntary surrender of it.

The citizenship of a naturalized person can be taken if it has been fraudulently obtained.

The original Constitution contained no provision with regard to the citizenship of native-born Americans, but did give Congress the right to naturalize aliens. The Fourteenth Amendment, however, declared that all persons "born or naturalized" in the United States were citizens both of the nation and of the state in which they resided.

Although the Constitution contained no provision giving Congress the right to take citizenship away, Congress has passed a considerable number of laws of that character. These covered a wide area: loss by marriage to a foreign man (not woman), voting in a foreign election, service in a foreign army, conviction of desertion in wartime, swearing allegiance to a foreign sovereign, and absence abroad with intent to evade the draft. Naturalized citizens might lose their citizenship by three years residence in the country of their birth, as well as by fraud in obtaining citizenship.

Congress has also made conviction for treason, for advocacy of the overthrow of the government by force, and for conspiracy to overthrow the government grounds for loss of American citizenship. These provisions have not yet been tested. Their constitutionality, except in the case of treason, is doubtful.

Until 1958 the Supreme Court had upheld the principle that Congress could legislate on the subject. In that year it decided three cases by divided votes. The Court ruled the provision valid that dealt with voting in a foreign election; it held that the provision with regard to service in a foreign army could not be applied to a person who had been drafted into that army. But it voided the provision that dealt with court-martial conviction for desertion.

That case involved a man, Trop, who, while in the army in North Africa in 1944 escaped into the desert from confinement for a minor offense, was arrested by military police

while on his way back to camp, was court-martialed for desertion and imprisoned. Many years after his release he applied
for a passport so as to be able to travel in connection with his
employment by an airline. He was refused the passport on the
ground that his conviction for desertion had forfeited his citizenship under a law passed during the Civil War. So he sued
the Secretary of State, lost in the lower courts, but won a 5 to
4 decision in the Supreme Court. The majority rested their
decision on the ground that there was no relation between
Trop's desertion and loss of allegiance to the country. Four of
the justices also thought that loss of nationality under these
circumstances constituted "cruel and unusual punishment"
(see section 43).

In 1963 the Court held that the section of the law which
took away citizenship for absence abroad to evade the draft
was unconstitutional because it did not give the person involved the safeguards contained in the Fifth and Sixth
Amendments. In the next year it voided the three-year provision that applied to naturalized citizens. Finally, in 1967 the
Court announced the rule that Congress had no power to take
away citizenship except for acts which clearly indicated that
the citizen intended to renounce his American nationality.
Justice Black said (387 U.S. 253):

> Citizenship is no light trifle to be jeopardized any moment Con-
> gress decides to do so under the name of one of its general or
> implied grants of power. In some instances, loss of citizenship
> can mean that a man is left without the protection of citizenship
> in any country in the world—as a man without a country. Citi-
> zenship in this Nation is a part of a cooperative affair. Its citi-
> zenry is the country and the country is its citizenry. The very
> nature of our free government makes it completely incongruous
> to have a rule of law under which a group of citizens temporar-
> ily in office can deprive another group of citizens of their citizen-
> ship. We hold that the Fourteenth Amendment was designed to,
> and does, protect every citizen of this Nation against a congres-
> sional forcible destruction of his citizenship, whatever his creed,

color, or race. Our holding does no more than to give to this
citizen that which is his own, a constitutional right to remain a
citizen in a free country unless he voluntarily relinquishes that
citizenship.

But in 1971 the Court, by a 5-4 vote, ruled that these earlier
decisions did not apply to conditions imposed on citizenship
created by Congress. Thus it upheld a law which caused a person born abroad of one American and one alien parent to lose
his American citizenship because he had not lived in the
United States for five years before reaching the age of 28.
The dissenters were Justices Black, Douglas, Brennan, and
Marshall.

Before a naturalized citizen can be deprived of his citizenship on the ground of alleged fraud in procuring it, the government must file an affidavit which contains facts sufficient
to show that it had probable cause to institute the proceeding.
Citizenship cannot be taken away for failure to disclose arrests for offenses which did not involve moral turpitude.

The Court ruled in 1943 that naturalization could not be
cancelled because the applicant had been a member of the
Communist party without proof that he had advocated the
overthrow of the government by force. The next year it held
that a German who had become naturalized while the Wei-
mar Republic was still the government of Germany did not
lose his naturalized status because he had made pro-Hitler
statements both before and after his naturalization.

14. Rights of Aliens

*Aliens are entitled to the protection of due process but are
subject to deportation without the protection of the prohibition
against ex post facto laws.*

It is traditional that a country has almost complete power to
deal with aliens. It can keep them out, deport them, and, in
time of war, intern enemy aliens. Nevertheless, in the United
States, aliens are generally protected by the due process and
equal protection clauses of the Fourteenth Amendment
against state action and by all the provisions of the Bill of
Rights against federal action. However, they have no rights
under the "privileges and immunities" clauses, as those protect only citizens. And in the vital matter of deportation an
alien is not protected by the prohibition against ex post facto
laws, as that relates only to punishments.

14a. *Exclusion*

An alien who is refused admission to the country has almost no rights. But if he has actually arrived in the country
and is detained by the immigration authorities he can try to
persuade the courts that he was entitled to entry in a habeas
corpus proceeding. In 1956 the Supreme Court ruled that he
could also bring an action to have his rights declared in court.
A Chinese alien had claimed that he was entitled to entry
under the War Brides Act passed in 1945 as the son of an
American who had served in the armed forces. In such situations the burden is on the alien to establish that he comes
within the provisions of some law which entitles him to enter
the United States.

In 1953 the Court, in two cases, passed on the right of the
Attorney General to bar aliens from entry without a hearing
or even giving any reason because, in his view, disclosure
might not be in the public interest. In the first case the Court
ruled that a seaman was entitled to a hearing, treating the
case as in effect a deportation proceeding, because the seaman's departure from the country had been for the purpose
of engaging in his vocation. But in the second the Court

reached a different conclusion where the alien had been absent for a visit abroad, even though the government had given up the idea of sending him out of the country because no other government would receive him and he was being indefinitely confined on Ellis Island.

In 1971 a three-judge court ruled, 2-1, that it was a violation of the First Amendment to refuse a visa to a Dr. Mandel, a Belgian Marxist, for the purpose of lecturing at various universities. The suit was brought by Dr. Mandel and several American university professors. The majority rested its decision primarily on the right of Americans to hear all points of view. The Supreme Court, however, held that the power of Congress over aliens was such that the Court should not interfere on supposed First Amendment grounds.

14b. *Deportation*

An alien who has entered the country is entitled to much greater rights. In all respects he has the same rights as a citizen when it comes to criminal prosecution or interference with his property. But in the matter of deportation his rights are more limited. He is entitled to a hearing and it must be a fair one. But if the decision to deport rests on some question of what the facts were, as distinguished from some interpretation of law or of the Constitution, the alien can get no redress in the courts.

Despite the severe consequences of deportation the Supreme Court has repeatedly held that it did not constitute punishment and therefore, that the prohibition against ex post facto legislation did not apply. So an alien can be deported under a law which makes some past act ground for deportation even though that act was not a ground for deportation when it was committed.

The law provides for the deportation of persons who, at time of entry, were "afflicted with psychopathic personality."

When this was applied to a homosexual the Court upheld his deportation on the ground that Congress had intended to include homosexuals within that description. Justices Douglas, Brennan, and Fortas dissented. Justice Douglas said (387 U.S. 118, 1967):

> It is common knowledge that in this century homosexuals have risen high in our own public service—both in Congress and in the Executive Branch—and have served with distinction. It is therefore not credible that Congress wanted to deport everyone and anyone who was a sexual deviate, no matter how blameless his social conduct had been nor how creative his work nor how valuable his contribution to society. I agree with Judge Moore, dissenting below, that the legislative history should not be read as imputing to Congress a purpose to classify under the heading "psychopathic personality" every person who ever had a homosexual experience.

Congress has made membership in an organization which advocates the overthrow of the government by force a ground for deportation. Under that law it is permissible to deport an alien member of such an organization without showing that he was a danger to the country. When Congress went even further and passed the Internal Security Act it made *past* membership in the Communist party a ground of deportation. The Supreme Court held this law to be constitutional but required a showing that the membership had been "meaningful." It reversed a deportation order because there was insufficient proof that the alien had been aware of the unlawful character of the party.

The law dealing with deportation gives the Attorney General discretion to suspend its provisions and permit the alien to stay here. The Supreme Court has been reluctant to interfere with his exercise of that discretion, even when he acted on the basis of confidential information which he refused to disclose. The Court ruled that the right to invoke that discretion was lost by an alien who claimed his privilege against self-incrimination when asked about Communist affiliations. In another case the Court held that an alien who had applied for relief from the draft could not qualify for the exercise of the Attorney General's discretion.

Chinese aliens who had been admitted to the country on parole while their right to enter was being litigated lost their case. They then tried to get the Attorney General to exercise his discretion on the ground that they would be subject to persecution if returned to Communist China. The Supreme Court refused to grant their request.

Problems have arisen in several cases where the country from which an alien had come has refused to let him return. Congress has made it a criminal offense for an alien in such a situation not to try to be admitted by some other country. While the Supreme Court upheld the constitutionality of this law it has ruled that to invoke it the government must show a willful failure on the part of the alien to do what the law required.

In one situation the Attorney General required aliens whose applications for the exercise of discretion he was considering to advise him of possible Communist activities and to restrict their activities in other ways. This the Supreme Court ruled was beyond his powers. But the Court has ruled that an alien might be kept in custody without bail pending the determination of his rights.

The Court ruled that an enemy alien could be deported without any hearing at all.

14c. *Naturalization*

Congress has provided for the naturalization of aliens under various conditions too elaborate for discussion here. The Supreme Court has had little occasion to pass on these provisions. The Court held that an alien who had claimed ex-

emption from the draft had not forfeited his right to apply
for citizenship. But an alien who falsely denied that he had
ever been a Communist could be refused citizenship even
without any proof that he had been a "meaningful" member
of the party.

14d. *State Regulation*

Many states deny aliens the right to practice certain
professions (such as law and medicine) and to enter certain
occupations. Such laws have been struck down when applied
in a discriminatory or arbitrary manner. In 1971 the Supreme
Court unanimously declared that state laws denying welfare
benefits to aliens or restricting them to long-term alien
residents violated the equal protection clause. In June 1973 it
condemned state restrictions on admission of aliens to the bar
and their employment in the civil service.

15. Rights of Labor

Until the 1930s the Supreme Court had generally been hostile
to labor unions. It upheld the imprisonment of Eugene V.
Debs (later several-time Socialist candidate for the Presidency) for contempt because he violated an injunction issued
against striking Pullman-car workers in the 1890s. The Court
approved injunctions which severely restricted the activities
of labor unions. It invalidated state and national laws that
outlawed "yellow dog" contracts and a state law that restricted the issuance of injunctions in labor disputes.

But, commencing with the passage by Congress of the Norris-La Guardia Act which restricted injunctions by federal
courts in labor disputes, the picture changed. The Supreme
Court upheld the law and has given it a liberal construction.
But the Court ruled that this law did not prevent the govern-

ment from getting an injunction against the United Mine
Workers during the time when the government was running
the mines after World War II.

The Supreme Court has also upheld the Wagner Act as a
proper exercise of congressional power over interstate commerce, and it has given the concept of such commerce a very
broad interpretation. The Court has thus upheld labor's right
to organize and to be free from employer harassment or discrimination because of union activities. This decision has not,
however, rested on any constitutional principle, so that
groups such as agricultural workers, who are not covered by
the act, have no rights. This fact particularly affects migrant
workers. The resulting problems led in the 1960s to activities
of the union in the Southwest led by Cesar Chávez, first in
connection with the picking of grapes, later with lettuce-pick-
ing.

15a. *Free Speech*

Early in the administration of the Wagner Act the problem
arose about an employer's right to express his views to his
employees: when was it constitutionally protected free
speech, when coercive and subject to restraint by the board
set up to administer the law? Congress amended the Wagner
Act so as to declare that an employer's expression of views
and opinions was not to be considered coercive by the National Labor Relations Board unless accompanied by threats
of reprisal or promise of benefits. In 1969 the Supreme Court
upheld a finding that various communications by an employer
had in fact been threats rather than expressions of opinion
because of their emphasis on the probability of the employees
being thrown out of work if a union called a strike to enforce
its demands. The decision rested primarily on the absence of
justification for the employer's statements that a strike
would follow unionization.

The right of labor leaders to free expression was involved in a challenge to the provision of the Taft-Hartley Act which barred unions from the benefits of the Wagner Act unless their officers filed affidavits that they were not members of the Communist party. While recognizing that this oath provision constituted a restriction on expression and association, the Court upheld it largely on the theory that the interference was slight. Congress, said the Court, had the right to take steps to prevent ill-disposed persons from controlling unions to foment political strikes.

15b. *Discrimination*

The Wagner Act clearly prohibits discrimination by employers against employees on account of their union activities and empowers the National Labor Relations Board to order the reinstatement of any employee discharged for such activities. No special problems have arisen in this area. But discrimination by unions is not dealt with in the law. It is notorious that many unions have discriminated against Negroes. Their right to do so has been restricted by a number of Supreme Court decisions.

The first of these arose under the Railway Labor Act. The union of firemen had collective bargaining agreements with railroads. These restricted the employment of firemen to persons who could be promoted and denied Negroes the right to promotion. In consequence many Negroes formerly employed as firemen lost their jobs. The Supreme Court condemned these agreements and ruled that no union recognized as representative of a group could use its power to deny employment or promotion to anyone on account of his race. The Court later held that the Norris-La Guardia Act did not prevent a federal court from enjoining such practices. The Court extended the principle of the earlier cases to a situation where a union used its bargaining power to prevent the employment of Negroes even though no Negroes had filled the particular positions described in the agreement.

15c. *State Regulation*

Since federal law is supreme in all areas over which Congress has power it follows that any state law which restricts a right given by federal law is void. Many problems of this kind have arisen in the field of labor relations. Since the Wagner Act recognizes the right to strike, a state cannot limit that right, as by requiring the vote of a majority of the workers in a plant, by compelling arbitration of the dispute, or by authorizing executive action to take over a utility if threatened with a strike.

State restrictions on picketing are permissible to the extent that the picketing is designed to accomplish an objective which is illegal under state law. This is so even if the law is not contained in a statute but has been laid down by the courts. There have been many instances. Thus in a state which requires employers to deal only with unions representing a majority of the workers peaceful picketing by a union that wants to force the employer to deal with it despite its minority status can be enjoined. The Supreme Court has also upheld an injunction issued by a state court against a union that tried to compel a parking-lot owner who had no employees to conform to union policy with regard to closing hours. The Court ruled that the state was free to protect the independence of self-employers against the demand of the union that its members be protected against the competition of nonunion persons.

But two New York injunctions were set aside. One restrained milk drivers from picketing producers who sold the milk and customers who bought it. The Supreme Court found this to be a legitimate activity of the union, noting that there had been no violence and little interference with strangers. In the other case the injunction rested on the use by pickets of signs containing false statements. The Supreme Court ruled this an interference with freedom of expression since the signs merely used the language of controversy.

Some years ago Texas tried to restrict union activity by requiring labor organizers to register and by prohibiting solicitation of union membership by persons who had not registered. R. J. Thomas, president of the CIO United Automobile Workers Union went to Texas to test the law and was met with an injunction, issued without any notice to him, which prohibited him from soliciting without first having registered. He ignored the injunction, addressed a meeting of workers, and asked the men to join his union. The Supreme Court set aside the state court's conviction for contempt on the ground that the injunction violated Thomas' right to freedom of expression.

On the other hand, the Court upheld the right of a state to outlaw the closed shop. It rejected the union's contention that the law violated its freedom of speech and assembly or denied it due process. Justice Black pointed out that the Supreme Court had abandoned the philosophy of cases decided early in the century which had denied legislative authority to deal with labor relations. He said (335 U.S. 525, 1949):

> Just as we have held that the due process clause erects no obstacle to block legislative protection of union members, we now hold that legislative protection can be afforded to non-union workers.

New York and New Jersey have entered into a compact (approved by Congress, as the Constitution requires) regulating the waterfront industry. The law forbids the collection of union dues for any union if any of its officers or agents have been convicted of a felony—though there are certain exemptions in the law. The Supreme Court upheld this law against challenge on free speech and due process grounds.

The Supreme Court ruled in 1969 that Louisiana had denied due process in setting up a commission for the purpose of publicly branding members of labor unions as violators of the criminal law because no opportunity was given to persons being investigated either to cross-examine hostile witnesses or to present evidence on their own behalf.

16. Rights of Witnesses Before Committees

The practice of obtaining information by calling persons before committees established by Congress and the various state legislative bodies is very old. Many such committees have performed valuable service in exposing corruption or inefficiency in the public administration. Others have delved into abuses by private persons or businesses and been responsible for important reform legislation. Laws such as the Wagner Act, the Federal Reserve Act, and the Securities Acts were enacted after extensive hearings in the areas of labor management, banking, and speculation. Without the publicity attendant on these hearings these laws would probably never have been passed.

Generally the committees call witnesses who are experts in their fields. Often they let any interested persons or organizations testify, or at least submit a statement expressing their views. But sometimes the committees call persons who are unwilling to testify or to give the desired information. Most committees have the power to subpoena witnesses and to punish recalcitrant witnesses for contempt. Sometimes a willful refusal to answer is punishable as a crime.

In investigations relating to offenses against the national

security by treason, sabotage, or sedition, witnesses can be compelled to testify by grant of immunity voted by two thirds of the members of the full committee provided a United States District Court enters an order to that effect on notice to the Attorney General.

Committees often hold sessions in private. These are known as "executive" sessions. In most instances testimony privately given is later made public, though with deletions in the interest of national security when such a problem arises.

16a. *Federal Committees*

The United States Supreme Court was repeatedly asked to rule on challenges to the power of the House Committee on Un-American Activities and the Senate subcommittee on Internal Security when they inquired into the Communist affiliation of people in the motion-picture industry, labor unions, and the academic world. At first it refused to exercise its discretionary power to review federal convictions for contempt, particularly in the cases of the writers known as the Hollywood Ten.

The basic challenge to the inquiries was based on the First Amendment: the inquiries infringed freedom of expression and of association. The House committee was also challenged on the ground that the resolution creating it was vague: no one could know what would be considered "Un-American."

Beginning with 1955 the Supreme Court reviewed many of these convictions. It reversed a few, generally on technical grounds, but rejected the basic constitutional challenges. In an early case Chief Justice Warren reminded Congress that its powers to investigate were not absolute, saying (349 U.S. 155):

But the power to investigate, broad as it may be, is also subject to recognized limitations. It cannot be used to inquire

148

into private affairs unrelated to a valid legislative purpose. Nor
does it extend to an area in which Congress is forbidden to legislate. Similarly, the power to investigate must not be confused
with any of the powers of law enforcement; those powers are
assigned under our Constitution to the Executive and the Judiciary. Still further limitations on the power to investigate are
found in the specific individual guarantees of the Bill of Rights,
such as the Fifth Amendment's privilege against self-incrimination which is an issue here.

The Court laid down the rule that the witness must be specifically directed to answer the particular question to which
he objected and that he was entitled to be clearly informed of
the bearing of the questions asked on the committee's inquiry—at least in the case of the House committee, because
of the broad scope of the resolution under which it acted.

One argument made by the recalcitrant witnesses was that
they were being questioned only in order to expose them to
loss of jobs and other disabilities, particularly as in most cases
the committees had received the information they were after
from willing witnesses, many of them ex-Communists.

In the *Watkins* case, decided in 1957, Chief Justice Warren
appeared to agree that committees could not inquire merely
to expose. He said (354 U.S. 178):

Abuses of the investigative process may imperceptibly lead to
abridgment of protected freedoms. The mere summoning of a
witness and compelling him to testify, against his will, about his
beliefs, expressions or associations is a measure of governmental interference. And when those forced revelations concern
matters that are unorthodox, unpopular, or even hateful to the
general public, the reaction in the life of the witness may be dis-
astrous. This effect is even more harsh when it is past beliefs,
expressions or associations that are disclosed and judged by current standards rather than those contemporary with the matters exposed.

But two years later the Court ruled otherwise in the *Barenblatt* case. There a record of statements made in reports issued by the House Committee on Un-American Activities to the effect that its objective was to expose Communists was presented to the Court. Nevertheless the conviction was affirmed. Justice Harlan refused to examine the motives of the committee; it was decisive that the committee had expressed a legitimate legislative purpose for its inquiry. He said (360 U.S. 109):

> Nor can we accept the further contention that this investigation should not be deemed to have been in furtherance of a legislative purpose because the true objective of the Committee and of the Congress was purely "exposure." So long as Congress acts in pursuance of its constitutional power, the Judiciary lacks authority to intervene on the basis of the motives which spurred the exercise of that power.

Justice Black dissented on the ground that the resolution under which the committee was acting was unconstitutionally vague, that First Amendment rights were being infringed, and that the House committee's objective was the impermissible one of exposure. He annexed to his opinion some of the statements from reports issued by the committee that indicated that its objective was to expose Communists. Chief Justice Warren and Justice Douglas joined in this dissent. Justice Brennan joined only with respect to the exposure issue. Justice Black said:

> It is the protection from arbitrary punishments through the right to a judicial trial with all these safeguards which over the years has distinguished America from lands where drumhead courts and other similar "tribunals" deprive the weak and the unorthodox of life, liberty and property without due process of law. It is this same right which is denied to Barenblatt, because the Court today fails to see what is here for all to see—that exposure and punishment is the aim of this Committee and the

reason for its existence. To deny this is to ignore the Committee's own claims and the reports it has issued ever since it was established. I cannot believe that the nature of our judicial office requires us to be so blind, and must conclude that the Un-American Activities Committee's "identification" and "exposure" of Communists and suspected Communists, like the activities of the Committee in *Kilbourn* v. *Thompson,* amount to an encroachment on the judiciary which bodes ill for the liberties of the people of this land.

In two later cases the Court upheld convictions for contempt despite the plea of the convicted men that they had been called for questioning only because they had been active opponents of the House Committee. The Court found enough evidence of possible Communist connections in testimony given to the committee about the two defendants to justify it in questioning them. Again Justice Black dissented and was again joined by Chief Justice Warren and Justices Douglas and Brennan. Justice Black said (365 U.S. 431, 1961):

The very foundation of a true democracy and the foundation upon which this Nation was built is the fact that government is responsive to the views of its citizens, and no nation can continue to exist on such a foundation unless its citizens are wholly free to speak out fearlessly for or against their officials and their laws. When it begins to send its dissenters, such as Barenblatt, Uphaus, Wilkinson, and now Braden, to jail, the liberties indispensable to its existence must be fast disappearing. If self-preservation is to be the issue that decides these cases, I firmly believe they must be decided the other way. Only by a dedicated preservation of the freedoms of the First Amendment can we hope to preserve our Nation and its traditional way of life.

Several persons were convicted for contempt for failing to produce records subpoenaed by a congressional committee. In one case the Court upheld the conviction of a woman who was one of eighteen members of the board of the organization whose records the committee wanted to see, despite testimony that she had no access to the records. The Court ruled that she should have attempted to get them. In a later case the contempt conviction was again sustained over the contention that the government had failed to show that the person subpoenaed had any control over the records. In that case, which was a 5 to 4 decision, the majority noted that a person with the same name as the witness was executive secretary of the organization involved and that the witness had made no attempt to explain.

16b. *State Committees*

Similar problems have arisen in connection with state investigating committees. Some of these have questioned unwilling witnesses about their Communist affiliations. Others, particularly in the South, have harassed organizations, such as the NAACP, which have been active in the support of Negroes' rights.

The Supreme Court reversed a New Hampshire conviction for contempt on the ground that the pertinency of the questions had not been established. Later it upheld a New Hampshire conviction for refusing, in an inquiry into Communist activities, to give the names of persons attending a certain camp. The second case was distinguished from the first on the ground that no question of academic freedom was now involved and also because the state had valid reason for supposing that some of the persons connected with the camp were Communists. In still another case from New Hampshire the contempt conviction was reversed because the questions related to the remote past and no showing had been made of any present danger to the state sufficient to justify such remote questioning.

Several Ohio contempt convictions were reversed because

the state committee had led the witnesses to believe that they could rely on their privilege against self-incrimination, only to find that the state court rejected that plea on the ground that they had received immunity.

An interesting case was decided in 1969. Louisiana created a commission to investigate violations of law by labor organizations. A labor organizer sued to enjoin enforcement of the law on the ground that it denied due process. The Supreme Court upheld his contention on the ground that the law in effect authorized condemnation without the safeguards of the criminal law. Justice Marshall said (395 U.S. 411):

> When viewed from this perspective, it is clear that the procedures of the Commission do not meet the minimal requirements made obligatory on the States by the Due Process Clause of the Fourteenth Amendment. Specifically, the Act severely limits the right of a person being investigated to confront and cross-examine the witnesses against him. Only a person appearing as a witness may cross-examine other witnesses. Cross-examination is further limited to those questions which the Commission deems appropriate to its inquiry. . . . We have frequently emphasized that the right to confront and cross-examine witnesses is a fundamental aspect of procedural due process. In the present context, where the Commission allegedly makes an actual finding that a specific individual is guilty of a crime, we think that due process requires the Commission to afford a person being investigated the right to confront and cross-examine the witnesses against him.

17. Rights of Vagrants

There are laws against vagrancy in almost every community. The definitions of vagrancy vary. Generally speaking they are aimed at persons without visible means of support, at beggars, at persons in masquerade, and at loiterers. These laws are often used by the police as justification for picking up anyone who looks to them like an undesirable or suspicious character. Challenges of these laws on the ground of vagueness have had varying results. In 1971 the Supreme Court reversed a conviction based on a charge of being a "suspicious" person and another for "loitering."

In 1972 the Court unanimously held an ordinance of Jacksonville, Florida, unconstitutionally vague. It prohibited "prowling by auto," "loitering," being a "common thief," and "disorderly loitering." The Court stressed the wide reach of the ordinance and the discretion it gave the police.

18. Freedom from Bills of Attainder

One of the few instances in which the Constitution itself restricted both the federal government and the states is the prohibition against the passage of bills of attainder in Article 1, Section 9, Clause 3, and in Section 10.

A bill of attainder is a legislative declaration of guilt. In England Parliament had often condemned men for treason, with resulting forfeiture of property, banishment, even death.

The Supreme Court has had few occasions to deal with that subject. It condemned laws passed after the Civil War by Congress and various state legislatures which attempted to disqualify persons from practicing their professions without taking an oath that they had not participated in the rebellion. In 1946 the Court also struck down an attempt by Congress to disqualify certain named individuals from federal employment.

On the other hand, in 1950 it upheld a provision of the Taft-Hartley Act which prevented a union from receiving the benefits of that law unless their officers swore that they were not Communists. The Court pointed out that if officers who had been Communists renounced their connection the disability would end. But in 1965 the Court voided a provision of a new law which prohibited persons from serving on the executive boards of unions if they had been members of the Communist party at any time during the past five years.

While ordinarily any penalty based on past action is prohibited by the Constitution, that rule does not apply where there is a reasonable relation between the past act and the penalty, as where a person who has been convicted of crime is disqualified from holding a position. The same rationale has been applied in connection with the part of the same constitutional provision dealing with ex post facto laws (see section 19).

19. Freedom from Ex Post Facto Laws

You cannot be convicted for any act that was not legally a crime when you committed it, or given more severe punishment than was legal for the act at that time.

The same clauses of the Constitution just discussed prohibit state and federal governments from passing ex post facto laws. The Founding Fathers had learned from English experience that the substance of justice could be denied when acts or words were made criminal after the event or when a greater punishment was inflicted than had been possible when the act was committed. Indeed, the value of the constitutional prohibition was pointed up in Nazi Germany, as when the burning of the Reichstag in 1933 was made high treason after the event.

The post-Civil War laws discussed in section 18 were also held void as ex post facto. Some laws disqualify applicants from the right to practice certain professions or trades because they have been convicted of acts which had not constituted such disqualification when they were performed. The ex post facto rule has not been applied in such cases if the act had a reasonable relation to the qualification.

The Court has enforced the prohibition also on increases in punishment but has ruled that mere procedural changes are not barred. As we have seen (section 14b), this prohibition does not apply to the deportation of aliens as deportation has not been considered punishment.

20. Right to a Clean Environment

The modern world has become very conscious of the problems of ecology. Pollution of air and water resulting from nuclear blasts, industrial exhausts and wastes, not to mention automobile fumes, have awakened many people to the need for action. Inroads on wilderness and marsh areas have aroused conservationists. The strong objection in New York to the building of an atomic plant by Consolidated Edison near Storm King Mountain brought together both groups of protesters, as did resistance to the encroachment of the Miami airport on the Everglades. The right of citizens to challenge projects they deem harmful to the community is being tested in a number of lawsuits. The outcome is, however, still uncertain as the Supreme Court has only begun to deal with the issues.

In its first decision in this field the Supreme Court, in March 1971, upheld the claim of conservationists that the courts should review administrative decisions challenged for lack of compliance with standards laid down by Congress. The Secretary of Transportation had approved construction of a highway through a park in Memphis, Tennessee. A group of citizens sued, contending that the Secretary had not complied with an act of Congress which permitted such interference with a park only when it caused "minimal" damage. The lower federal courts threw their suit out. The Supreme Court reversed these decisions and ruled that there must be a hearing at which the Secretary would have to explain his action and show that it was not arbitrary.

But a few weeks later the Court refused to exercise the power given to it by the Constitution to hear, in the first instance, suits by states in a case brought by the State of Ohio against several chemical companies to stop pollution of Lake Erie. The Court ruled that this was a matter for the state courts.

By a vote of 4 to 3 the Court refused to stay the atomic detonation which took place on Amchitka Island on November 6, 1971. Justices Douglas, Brennan, and Marshall thought a stay should have been granted so that the Court could determine whether there had been compliance with the laws governing such tests.

In April 1973 the Court handed down a number of decisions which opened the door to litigation in this field. It refused to take original jurisdiction in suits by states against private concerns or municipalities but did take a case in which there were states on each side, even though a private concern was also a defendant. The Court pointed out that lower federal courts had jurisdiction to ban pollution as a common nuisance. Earlier the Court had ruled, 4-3, that the Sierra Club could not sue to challenge the Disney project in Mineral King Valley, California, because it had not claimed that any of its members were threatened with injury by the project. Justices Douglas, Brennan, and Blackmun dissented.

Right to
Due Process of Law

This right rests on the due process clauses of the Fifth and Fourteenth Amendments, the first binding only on the federal government, the second binding on the states. It is through the latter that almost all of the specific provisions of the Bill of Rights, such as freedom of expression, freedom of assembly, freedom of religion, freedom from unreasonable searches and seizures, and the right to bear arms, have been made applicable to the states. The others, which deal mostly with criminal prosecutions, follow: protection against double jeopardy, protection against self-incrimination, the requirement of indictment, the right to trial by jury, the right to confront witnesses, the right to counsel, protection against cruel and unusual punishment, and the right to have reasonable bail.

Two other protections, contained in the body of the Constitution, which are binding on both state and federal governments have already been analyzed: the prohibition of bills of attainder and of ex post facto laws.

21. Basic Procedures

The right of any person not to be "deprived of life, liberty or property, without due process of law" is guaranteed against federal action by the Fifth Amendment and, since 1868, against state action by the Fourteenth Amendment. These provisions have most often been invoked in review of convictions for crime. But there are various other procedural guarantees of the federal Bill of Rights. Originally binding only on the federal government, now almost all of them also restrict the states.

The major steps in criminal proceedings are arrest, arraignment, certain intermediate steps, trial, and, often, appeal.

21a. *Arrest*

The moment a person knows that he is suspected of having committed a crime he should be aware of his rights. Basic is the proposition that he doesn't have to answer any questions put by a policeman or investigating officer. But until the person being questioned is actually in custody, if he does talk freely what he says can later be used against him, even if he was not warned of his right to remain silent.

One can, of course, be taken into custody by any policeman, some federal agents and, in certain circumstances, even by an ordinary citizen. The question of whether the arrest was lawful does not affect the right of the government to bring the person arrested to trial, but it can have other consequences. Statements made or things seized at the time of arrest cannot be used at the trial if the arrest was unlawful. The arresting officer can also be sued for damages. So it is often important to determine whether an arrest was legal.

A word of caution is in order. It seldom pays to get into an argument with a policeman who is arresting you or, for that matter, with one who is arresting someone else. In the first instance you may be beaten up for your daring; in the second you are likely to be arrested yourself on a charge of interfering with the officer's performance of his duty. It can even be dangerous to ask a policeman to tell you his name or shield number. So when tempted to assert your rights at the time of arrest remember the jingle:

> Here lies the body of Thomas Gray
> Killed for insisting on his right of way.

The wisest course, however unpalatable, is meekly to submit to the arrest and let your lawyer do the arguing. Not that a lawyer is necessarily immune to police harassment, but police annoyance at him will not usually result in harm to you.

Obviously, anyone who is arrested should at once try to get a lawyer, one of his own choice if he can pay for him, a volunteer or state-provided lawyer if he cannot. There are many organizations ready to provide lawyers free of charge when constitutional rights are involved: the local affiliates of the American Civil Liberties Union, or chapters of the National Association for the Advancement of Colored People or of the National Lawyers Guild. In many communities there are Legal Aid Societies, in some there are Public Defenders selected and paid by the community.

Arrests can legally be made without a warrant under certain situations. These differ from state to state. Generally it can be said that a police officer or even a private person can arrest for any crime committed in his presence, and that an officer can make an arrest for a felony he has reason to believe was committed by the suspect. In 1968 the Supreme Court upheld arrests by policemen who had stopped persons they believed endangered their safety or that of others.

When the arrest is made under a warrant it can be challenged if the papers on which it was obtained are defective. These must state facts that connect the person to be arrested with a specific offense, not merely with suspicions or legal conclusions (see section 4a).

Once in custody—and that need not be by way of formal arrest—the situation changes radically. In the famous *Miranda* case in 1966 the Supreme Court ruled that no statement taken from a person in custody could later be used against him unless certain safeguards were employed: the suspect must be told he need not say anything and that if he does talk what he says can be used against him; that he has a right to get a lawyer and that if he is unable to hire one he will be provided with one. But even if all these safeguards have been observed, no statement can be used if obtained by force, threats, or promises (see section 27).

The right to have a lawyer in a federal prosecution is expressly guaranteed by the Sixth Amendment (see section 34b). But the right to have a lawyer for defense in a state prosecution developed slowly. At first, in the Scottsboro case of 1932 the Supreme Court confined that right to persons accused of a crime punishable by death. Then the Court ruled that counsel must be provided whenever the circumstances indicated that it would otherwise be unfair to the defendant because of his youth, his inexperience, or the complexities of the charge against him. For years the Court divided sharply in deciding particular cases and created such uncertainty that when the crucial *Gideon* case came along in 1963 the highest legal officers of most states urged the Court to abandon its earlier position and to rule that counsel must be provided by the states in all criminal cases. And the Court did just that, excepting minor offenses such as traffic violations.

21b. *Arraignment*

After a person has been arrested he is arraigned, that is, taken before a judge. This is supposed to be done at once—a rule more honored in the breach than the observance. The police like to question a suspect before he gets a chance to get bail from a judge. But undue delay in bringing a person before a judge may result in upsetting a conviction. And failure to provide a lawyer will bar use of any statements obtained.

When the suspect is arraigned he is supposed to plead guilty or not guilty. Often the pleading is delayed for one reason or another. It is important to have a lawyer promptly because only a lawyer knows what steps should be taken for the protection of the suspect, and what motions to make, as for particulars. The Supreme Court has not, however, required that a suspect be provided with a lawyer at the time of arraignment unless some rights might be lost by failure to assert them then.

The suspect should try to be released on his own "recognizance," that is, on his promise to appear when the case is next called. If that is refused he should try to get as low bail as possible.

21c. *Intermediate Steps*

There are many things a lawyer can do between arraignment and trial. If the arrest occurred before the case had been considered by a grand jury the lawyer usually asks for a preliminary hearing so that he can cross-examine the witnesses produced by the prosecution and, perhaps, get the case dismissed.

After there has been an indictment the lawyer may ask to see the grand-jury minutes in order to determine whether or not there was sufficient evidence before the grand jury to warrant a prosecution. In some states a defendant is entitled to see these minutes; in others he gets them only if a judge thinks he should. Sometimes the judge will look at the minutes without letting the defense lawyer see them and will dismiss the indictment if he finds there was insufficient evidence. In the federal courts inspection of grand-jury minutes is rarely allowed.

If the defendant knows that there has been a search which might have turned up evidence harmful to him he should tell his lawyer so that the lawyer can move to suppress the evidence if he can show that the search was illegal (see section 4a). So if the defendant has reason to believe that there had been wiretapping or other eavesdropping the lawyer will ask for a hearing to find out just what was learned and likewise move to suppress (see section 4b).

21d. *Trial*

The first question to be decided is whether the defendant is entitled to a jury trial. The Sixth Amendment expressly requires that a jury be called in all criminal cases. For a long time the Supreme Court held that this requirement applied only to trials in federal courts. But in 1968 the Court imposed it also on the states. Then came the question of whether there were offenses that could be tried without the participation of a jury.

Long ago the Court held that Congress could authorize federal trials by a judge alone in a case involving minor offenses: those punishable by imprisonment other than at hard labor. In 1970 the Court ruled that there must be jurors in all cases, even prosecutions for misdemeanors, where the possible imprisonment could exceed six months.

Many states give the jury discretion whether or not to impose the death penalty for various crimes. In some states the jury makes that determination at the same time that it passes on guilt or innocence. In May 1971 the Supreme Court upheld the right of the states both to give discretion to the jury and to permit that discretion to be exercised at the same time as the jury renders its verdict. In 1972 the Court ruled, 5-4, that capital punishment as practiced in most states is unconstitutional, a "cruel and unusual punishment" too often reserved for the powerless, especially the poor and Negroes.

Although there is nothing in the original Constitution or any of the amendments that says so, it is fundamental to the Anglo-American legal system that a person charged with crime is presumed to be innocent. That means that the prosecution must establish its case by competent evidence and that the defendant can remain silent.

However, like almost all statements about the law this one has its exceptions. There are limited situations in which, if a defendant offers no explanation, some important element of the crime charged can be established without direct proof of it by the prosecution. A common instance is possession of property that has recently been stolen. When the fact of theft is proved by the prosecution it will be presumed that the defendant knew the property had been stolen unless he can explain how he came to have it. This occurs also when a legislature or the Congress has enacted a law which creates a presumption that a certain fact will be taken as proved unless the defendant explains it away. There are many such laws, some of which have been declared unconstitutional for lack of a rational relation between the fact actually proved and the fact sought to be established by use of the presumption. An example is a federal law which presumed that anyone who could not explain his possession of a drug was aware that it had been illegally imported. The Supreme Court upheld the application of this law to certain drugs but not to others (see section 38).

In every criminal case the prosecution must also establish

the defendant's guilt "beyond a reasonable doubt." Juries are instructed that this does not mean they can acquit a defendant merely because they have some doubt. It must be such a doubt as a reasonable man would have in reaching conclusions in his ordinary activities. Even if a jury has been properly instructed on this matter, convictions are sometimes set aside by appellate courts on the ground there was not enough evidence in the case to justify a finding of guilt beyond a reasonable doubt.

21e. *Appeal*

To get an appellate court to review a conviction a prompt appeal must be made. This must usually be done within a very short period. In federal courts this is ten days. Failure to appeal is almost always fatal, but exceptions do occur. If a convict is indigent he is entitled to have the stenographer's minutes and other material necessary for his appeal furnished by the state without expense and to file his papers without paying a fee. In 1963 the Court held that the state must also give him a lawyer to handle the appeal. It must be a lawyer who acts as an advocate. In one case the lawyer appointed by the state court refused to go ahead with the appeal because he thought it had no merit; the Supreme Court said a different lawyer should have been provided.

In both federal and state systems there is one appeal "as of right," that is, without the permission of the higher court being necessary except in a few instances where only a small fine has been imposed.

A person convicted of crime in either state or federal court, after he has exhausted all the avenues of appeal ordinarily available, comes as a last resort to the United States Supreme Court—or to be more accurate, he tries to get there by appeal or certiorari, for it is not easy to get that Court to act. The

Court can review a state conviction only if a claim of deprivation of some federally guaranteed right, either under the
Constitution, treaty, or act of Congress, was raised and considered in a lower court.

If an appeal is disposed of, even summarily, the result ends
the case. But denial of certiorari need not do so. The Supreme
Court has made it clear that denial of certiorari does not constitute a decision on the merits of the case. As Justice Frankfurter pointed out in 1950, denial of certiorari means only
that four justices did not think the case should be heard on its
merits. He listed among the considerations which influenced
the justices (338 U.S. 912):

> Narrowly technical reasons may lead to denials. Review may
> be sought too late; the judgment of the lower court may not be
> final; it may not be the judgment of a State court of last resort;
> the decision may be supportable as a matter of State law, not
> subject to review by this Court, even though the State court
> also passed on issues of federal law. A decision may satisfy all
> these technical requirements and yet may commend itself for
> review to fewer than four members of the Court. Pertinent con-
> siderations of judicial policy here come into play. A case may
> raise an important question but the record may be cloudy. It
> may be desirable to have different aspects of an issue further il-
> lumined by the lower courts. Wise adjudication has its own time
> for ripening.

Even if certiorari has been denied by the Supreme Court, or
if a conviction has been upheld by an evenly divided Supreme
Court, a person convicted in a state court and either imprisoned or facing the possibility of later imprisonment, can
apply to a federal court for a writ of habeas corpus and there
reargue the federal constitutional issue which had been
unsuccessfully presented to the Supreme Court earlier. The
Supreme Court may then take the case. This may happen
because issues were more clearly presented at the second
hearing, because other cases raising the same constitutional

point had come up, or because of a change in the membership of the Court. It is not possible to explain the various instances by any general rule. Now, however, the first step is no longer necessary, so that an attempt to review an unfavorable habeas corpus decision need not have behind it the denial of certiorari on direct review.

Many of the most far-reaching decisions in the field of civil liberties have been made in review of habeas corpus cases. In some cases relief was granted many years after the conviction—twenty years in one case. This remedy of habeas corpus is, however, not available to a person who has had his sentence suspended or merely been fined. Only a person in custody or under serious restrictions on his freedoms can obtain the writ.

This ancient writ of habeas corpus is one of the great glories of Anglo-American jurisprudence. The term literally means to "have the body" (of a person in custody) brought before the court. The court can thus pass on the legality of his confinement. (The writ is also used to test the custody of children and the confinement of persons in mental institutions.) It is one of the vital protections against arbitrary power. Its availability makes it impossible for our government to keep anyone in confinement without legal cause.

A decision by the lower court either granting or refusing the writ of habeas corpus can be appealed to the Court of Appeals, with the permission of either court. Finally the case can come to the Supreme Court if it thinks the issue important enough to grant certiorari.

The bulk of petitions for certiorari to the Supreme Court in these habeas corpus cases are presented by indigent prisoners who ask to be permitted to proceed *in forma pauperis*. That means they do not have to pay filing fees, can present typewritten papers, and if successful have the record and their brief printed at government expense. If, as very often is the case, the papers were drawn by the convict without legal as-

sistance, the Supreme Court will appoint counsel to prepare
the final brief and argue the case. These convict-drawn papers often present difficulties because of the inexpert way
they are prepared.

The Constitution itself prohibits any suspension of the writ
of habeas corpus except in time of invasion or rebellion. We
have had few occasions in our history to suspend the writ (see
section 6).

22. Early State Cases

Early in the nineteenth century several attempts were made
to get the United States Supreme Court to review state convictions on the theory that they violated some guarantee of
the Bill of Rights. All such attempts failed because the Court
ruled that the Bill of Rights restricted the federal government alone. Only where the Court found that a state violated
one of the few restrictions on its action as were contained in
the Constitution itself, such as denial of the power to pass
bills of attainder or ex post facto laws (see sections 18, 19), did
the Court consider the merits of the claims that were asserted.

After the adoption of the Fourteenth Amendment in 1868
the picture changed altogether because that amendment expressly deprived the states of the right to deny due process
(and also equal protection [see section 9]). But it was a long
time before the Supreme Court actually reversed a state conviction on the ground that it had denied the defendant due
process of law. The first instance occurred in 1923. The Court
found that the trial of certain Arkansas Negroes had been no
more than mockery because of the claim that it had been conducted under the dictates of a threatening mob. The Court
therefore ordered a hearing to ascertain the truth. Justice
Holmes said (261 U.S. 86):

But if the case is that the whole proceeding is a mask—that counsel, jury and judge were swept to the fatal end by an irresistible wave of public passion, and that the State Courts failed to correct the wrong, neither perfection in the machinery for correction nor the possibility that the trial court and counsel saw no other way of avoiding an immediate outbreak of the mob can prevent this Court from securing to the petitioners their constitutional rights.

23. Vague Laws

One of the fundamental concepts of due process is that a person should know what conduct he might engage in that would subject him to criminal prosecution. Therefore a law which is so general that it might embrace conduct not inherently wrongful or which uses words not easily defined can be attacked as too vague. The Supreme Court has dealt with many such cases. Years ago it ruled too vague a law which prohibited "unreasonable" charges. So in 1939 the Court held too vague a New Jersey law which punished "gangsters." In 1948 the Court voided a New York conviction of the publisher of a magazine charged with the distribution of matter which contained accounts of crime and bloodshed. As we have already noted (see section 1q), many laws prescribing oaths have been struck down as too vague.

In May 1971, the Court reversed the conviction of a man charged as being a "suspicious" person and of another for "loitering."

24. Entrapment

The claim is sometimes made by a defendant that he was "entrapped" by a government agent or informer into committing

the crime charged. This defense is seldom successful as the
defendant must show that he was really induced to commit
the crime by some kind of pressure or persistence. It is not
enough to show only that an opportunity to commit it was
created by the agent or informer. The Supreme Court said in
the *Sherman* case that distinction should be made "between
the trap for the unwary innocent and the trap for the unwary
criminal." In that case a government informer had met the
defendant at a doctor's office where both were being cured
for addiction. The informer asked the defendant to get some
narcotics and persisted in his efforts after the defendant
showed reluctance. There was no evidence, except for convictions many years earlier, that the defendant was in the business of dealing in narcotics. The Supreme Court reversed the
conviction. Chief Justice Warren said (356 U.S. 369, 1958):

> The function of law enforcement is the prevention of crime and
> the apprehension of criminals. Manifestly, that function does
> not include the manufacturing of crime. Criminal activity is
> such that stealth and strategy are necessary weapons in the ar-
> senal of the police officer. However, "A different question is pre-
> sented when the criminal design originates with the officials of
> the Government, and they implant in the mind of an innocent
> person the disposition to commit the alleged offense and induce
> its commission in order that they may prosecute." [287 U.S., at
> 442.] Then stealth and strategy become as objectionable police
> methods as the coerced confession and the unlawful search.

This problem is likely to arise in situations where government agents have infiltrated groups which the government
thinks might be involved in criminal activity. Sometimes such
agents do more than merely observe and report possible violations of law. Often they take an active part in the activities
they have been sent to watch. Indeed, the history of all revolutionary movements is replete with claims that government
agents have themselves violated the law, even induced others
to do so. Such persons have been called "agents provoca-

teurs." Whether their activities permit a defendant to claim entrapment will depend on the particular facts of each case, measured by the rule of the *Sherman* case, just quoted.

But the defense of entrapment is never available unless the defendant admits that he committed the acts charged.

25. Informants

You are entitled to know the identity of an informant when this is essential to the protection of your rights.

It is, of course, a commonplace for police to use informants to get tips about the possible commission of a crime or the identity of the person who has done a criminal act. If such informant becomes a witness at the trial, his identity will naturally be disclosed. But generally that is not the case. The information obtained is used as the basis of getting a warrant of arrest or a search warrant or, in some cases, to justify an arrest without a warrant (see section 4a). And in these situations the identity of the informant is generally withheld. Decisions on the subject have not been altogether consistent.

In the *Roviaro* case a man was charged with having sold and transported narcotics. Testimony was given by government agents who observed the sale. They refused to identify the person to whom the sale had been made on the ground that he was an informer. The Supreme Court held that wherever refusal to disclose such information was prejudicial to the defense, the government must either give it or drop the prosecution. Here the majority found prejudice and ordered a new trial.

The Court avoided passing on the necessity for disclosing the identity of an informant in one case because the request had been made only in connection with a challenge to a search warrant and not in relation to the trial on the merits.

171

26. Identification

The police when they try to get the victim of or witness to a crime to identify a suspect use various methods. Sometimes a photograph is shown, sometimes the suspect is produced for inspection; the most common practice is to put the suspect in a lineup. The Supreme Court has been critical when police let the witness see the suspect alone except under special circumstances, as when the witness is at death's door. The lineup procedure is improper if it is organized in such a way as to point the finger at the suspect. That was the situation where the suspect in a robbery case was much taller than the other men and had been forced to wear a jacket like the one worn by the robber. And if an indicted person had no lawyer at the lineup the Court has ruled that the prosecution must show that any identification made at the trial was based on factors independent of the observation at the lineup.

27. Confessions

You can prevent the use of a confession obtained under duress or by physical force or mental coercion.
You cannot prevent the use of a confession freely given.

The Supreme Court in 1897 in the *Bram* case laid down the rule that no confession could be used at a federal criminal trial that had been obtained by force, threats, or promises.

It was a long time, however, before this doctrine was applied to a state conviction, despite growing concern over the use of "third-degree" measures by local police. That term referred to police brutality against prisoners after they were taken into custody and before they were arraigned in court in the hope of getting them to confess. But in 1936 the Court reversed a Mississippi conviction of three Negroes who had been tortured into confessing that they had murdered a white man. Chief Justice Hughes thus reviewed the requirements of due process (297 U.S. 278):

> The rack and torture chamber may not be substituted for the witness stand. The State may not permit an accused to be hurried to conviction under mob domination—where the whole proceeding is but a mask—without supplying corrective process. The State may not deny to the accused the aid of counsel. Nor may a State, through the action of its officers, contrive a conviction through the pretense of a trial which in truth is "but used as a means of depriving a defendant of liberty through a deliberate deception of court and jury by the presentation of testimony known to be perjured." And the trial equally is a mere pretense where the state authorities have contrived a conviction resting solely upon confessions obtained by violence.

State convictions have been reversed in a variety of cases where confessions were obtained that the Court found were not voluntary; where violence was used to extort the confession; where the defendant was held in custody for many days without opportunity to consult a lawyer; where he was under the influence of drugs; where he was kept in a "sweat box"; where a so-called truth serum had been injected into him. The same result was reached where the authorities refused to allow a prisoner to telephone his wife or lawyer unless he "cooperated" with the police, and in another case where they threatened to cut off state aid for a woman's children and to take them away from her.

In 1954 the Court was called on to consider the impact of what might be called mental rather than physical coercion. One Leyra, suspected of the murder of both parents, had been questioned in a New York City police station. When he complained of sinus pains the police captain said he would send in a doctor to help. The doctor sent was a psychiatrist who, for an hour and a half, tried to induce Leyra to confess. The conversation between Leyra and the doctor was wired to a room in which the captain listened, and was taped. When Leyra finally said he would talk to the captain the officer walked in and the doctor left. Confessions followed. At Leyra's first trial the tape and the confessions were put in evidence. New York's highest court reversed his first-degree murder conviction on the ground that the tape should have been excluded because the psychiatrist used mental coercion. It ruled that at the second trial the jury should determine whether the taint extended to the later confessions. The jury again convicted Leyra. New York's Court of Appeals upheld the conviction and the Supreme Court refused to review the case. Then a habeas corpus proceeding was commenced in a federal court on the ground that the confessions were so intimately connected with the impropriety committed by the psychiatrist that it was irrational and, therefore, a denial of due process to permit a jury to find otherwise. This time the Supreme Court heard the case and ruled there must be another trial. Justice Black said (347 U.S. 556):

> The undisputed facts in this case are irreconcilable with petitioner's mental freedom "to confess to or deny a suspected participation in a crime," and the relation of the confessions made to the psychiatrist, the police captain and the state prosecutors, is "so close that one must say the facts of one control the character of the other. . . ." All were simply parts of one continuous process. All were extracted in the same place within a period of about five hours as the climax of days and nights of intermittent, intensive police questioning. First, an already physically and emotionally exhausted suspect's ability to resist interrogation was broken to almost trance-like submission by use of the arts of a highly skilled psychiatrist. Then the confession petitioner began making to the psychiatrist was filled in and perfected by additional statements given in rapid succession to a police officer, a trusted friend, and two state prosecutors. We hold that use of confessions extracted in such a manner from a lone defendant unprotected by counsel is not consistent with due process of law as required by our Constitution.

(After the third trial at which no confessions were read to the jury and the jury convicted Leyra, New York's highest court reversed the conviction on the ground that without the confessions the evidence was insufficient for a finding of guilt beyond a reasonable doubt. Leyra went free.)

In 1964 the Court rendered a far-reaching decision in *Jackson* v. *Denno* to the effect that it is improper to ask a jury to consider the validity of a confession as part of its overall deliberations, since it is impossible for a reviewing court to determine whether the jury in convicting had rejected the confession and so rested its verdict on other evidence, or whether it had accepted a confession that should have been rejected. The Court ruled, therefore, that the trial judge should first pass on the voluntariness of the confession. The jury should be allowed to pass on its truthfulness only when the judge finds that it has been properly obtained.

In a very unusual situation the Court ruled in 1963 that relief could be obtained in a federal habeas corpus proceeding even though there had been no attempt to have the constitutional issue involved—the use of an illegally obtained confession—passed on by a state court on appeal. That result was reached because two codefendants who had unsuccessfully appealed in the state courts had been successful in getting new trials ordered by a federal court on the ground that their confessions, obtained under the same circumstances as the confession of a third defendant, had been illegally obtained.

In the federal courts confessions have been rejected on grounds not strictly constitutional because of the Supreme Court's supervisory power over those courts, as where arrested persons were held incommunicado for several days. In the *Mallory* case the Court reversed a conviction when confessions followed after a number of suspects had been detained for several hours and induced to take lie detector tests. Justice Frankfurter said (354 U.S. 449, 1957):

It is not the function of the police to arrest, as it were, at large and to use an interrogating process at police headquarters in order to determine whom they should charge before a committing magistrate on "probable cause."

The Court ruled, however, that a confession could be used even though it was obtained while the accused was in custody (after his arraignment) for an entirely different offense from the one to which the confession related. The Court at one time allowed the use of a confession given by one defendant that implicated his codefendant when the judge had made it clear to the jury that the confession could not be considered against the codefendant. But in 1968 this decision was expressly overruled and such use of a confession involving a codefendant was condemned. A different result was reached in 1971 where the codefendant had testified.

Since the *Miranda* decision of 1966 no statement given by a person in custody can be used against him unless he was warned that he could remain silent, that he had the right to have a lawyer with him, and that one would be provided for him if he was unable to pay for a lawyer.

In a 5–4 decision handed down in February 1971, the Court ruled that a statement taken from a person suspected of having committed a crime can be used by the prosecution to rebut testimony given at the trial even though it is not available to the prosecution as part of its case because the safeguards required by the *Miranda* case had not been observed. The majority rested their conclusion on a decision handed down in 1954 in which the Court had allowed the use of illegally seized material to contradict a defendant's testimony. Justices Black, Douglas, Brennan, and Marshall dissented.

28. Indictment

The government cannot prosecute a serious offense without getting an indictment from a grand jury.

The defendant cannot ordinarily find out what testimony the grand jury heard.

One of the guarantees contained in the Fifth Amendment requires that all prosecutions for capital or "infamous" crimes must be instituted by an indictment, which can be done only by a grand jury.

This guarantee of prosecution by indictment by a grand jury is not one of those which have been siphoned into the due process clause of the Fourteenth Amendment, so as to be construed as binding on the states. However, where indictment *is* the method approved by a state, discrimination in the selection of the grand jury becomes a federal question under the equal protection clause (see section 9b).

The institution of the grand jury is very old. It proved a useful barrier in England against persecution by royal authority. It continues to serve as a mitigator of the law's harshness. Many a person technically guilty is never indicted because the grand jury thinks the public interest would be better served by forgetting the incident than by prosecuting.

The proceedings of the grand jury are conducted in private. The person suspected of having committed a crime is ordinarily not called as a witness. No witness can bring his lawyer with him into the grand-jury room, but he can ask the right to consult his lawyer outside. In some states a practice has developed among defense lawyers of asking to see the grand-jury minutes in order to challenge the sufficiency of the evidence it relied on in bringing in an indictment. But in the federal courts this is rarely allowed.

When the gambler Frank Costello was charged with not reporting his true income he established that the only evidence before the grand jury was that of government agents who testified to the results of their investigations. He challenged the propriety of this on the ground that the agents had no personal knowledge of the matters involved. But the Supreme Court overruled that contention. The Court took the position that the ordinary rules of evidence did not apply to grand juries and that only discrimination in the selection of the jurors might be looked into.

But the United States Court of Appeals that sits in New York has on several occasions condemned the use of hearsay testimony before a grand jury when direct evidence was readily available. The Court questioned that the *Costello* decision was intended to deal with such a situation.

All crimes must be prosecuted by indictment if they are punishable by imprisonment in a penitentiary or at hard labor, regardless of the length of sentence or, perhaps, even the character of the crime. Thus a conviction without prior indictment for the offense of neglecting minor children was set aside because the punishment was at hard labor, whereas a conviction without indictment for intimidating a juror was upheld because the statute did not permit punishment at hard labor or incarceration in a penitentiary.

The guarantee applies to aliens but not to persons tried by military tribunal as spies. The extent to which the guarantee applies to Puerto Rico (and formerly applied to Hawaii and Alaska) is discussed hereafter in the section dealing with juries (see section 33).

In many states district attorneys can prosecute a great variety of crimes without submitting any evidence to a grand jury. They simply write out a charge—it is called an information. And in the few states that have no grand-jury system at all the usual way in which a criminal prosecution is commenced is by the filing of an information.

29. Bail

The Eighth Amendment prohibits the exaction of "excessive bail." This is not a guarantee of bail in all situations. The Supreme Court held in 1952 by a 5 to 4 vote that Congress had the right to authorize the Attorney General to hold alleged members of the Communist party without bail pending pro-

ceedings for their deportation. And bail has customarily been
denied in murder cases where the punishment might be
death.

But in 1951 the Court ruled that, where bail is allowed, it
must have a reasonable relation to the circumstances of the
case. Its prime purpose is to secure the defendant's attendance at trial and submission to any sentence that may be imposed on him.

Ordinarily, where a defendant believes that bail has been
set too high he should move in the criminal case to have it reduced rather than to institute habeas corpus proceedings to
have lower bail fixed.

30. Preventive Detention

The outcry against the increase in certain crimes has led to
the inclusion in the crime bill enacted by the Ninety-first Congress for the District of Columbia of a provision giving
judges the power to deny bail to a person suspected of a particular offense if his past record is such as to indicate that he
may do some criminal act while out on bail. This practice has
been described as "preventive detention." It runs counter to
the presumption of innocence and, where practiced, is sure to
be challenged. The remedy it is supposed to accomplish can,
most authorities agree, be better accomplished by cutting
down the time between arrest and trial.

31. Insanity

You cannot be forced to trial if insane.

It has long been an Anglo-American tradition that a person cannot be convicted if he was insane when he committed the offense or even put on trial for an offense if his mental condition is such that he cannot understand the nature of the charge against him and cooperate with his lawyer.

When a judge believes that a defendant is in the latter condition he usually orders a psychiatric examination. If that confirms the judge's belief, the defendant will be sent to an institution for the mentally ill. There have been many instances where a person charged with a relatively minor offense remains in the institution for many years and is never tried. The law on the rights of such persons is in the developing stage.

Some years ago the Supreme Court upheld such an order of confinement because of the medical testimony, pointing out that the defendant could ask for a writ of habeas corpus to test his condition at any time.

But the defense of insanity cannot be forced on a defendant. So the Supreme Court ruled in a District of Columbia case when the prosecution offered testimony, over defense objection, that the defendant had committed the offense as the result of mental illness and the court found him not guilty because insane and committed him to a mental hospital.

The standards for determining when a person is so mentally ill that he should not be held responsible have changed radically in some places in recent years. But the Supreme Court has not dealt with that subject.

32. Publicity

A conviction will not stand if the defendant was subjected to undue publicity before or during his trial.

The extent to which publicity affects the fairness of a trial has troubled the Court for some time. In 1961 it set aside a state conviction because the authorities had stimulated publicity adverse to the defendant and a change of venue had been refused. Another state conviction was reversed because of television showings of an interview with the defendant in which he made damaging admissions. Justice Stewart said (373 U.S. 723, 1963):

> Any subsequent court proceedings in a community so pervasively exposed to such a spectacle could be but a hollow formality.

Similar results were reached in the Texas case of Billie Sol Estes and the Ohio case of Dr. Sheppard. Estes was charged with swindling farmers to purchase fertilizer tanks and equipment which did not exist. There had been massive pretrial publicity. A defense motion to prevent telecasting and broadcasting resulted in a two-day hearing which was carried live by both media, with considerable resulting confusion. Justice Clark, himself a Texan, wrote the opinion (381 U.S. 532, 1965) and said:

> The potential impact of television on the jurors is perhaps of the greatest significance. They are the nerve center of the fact-finding process. It is true that in States like Texas where they are required to be sequestered in trials of this nature the jurors will probably not see any of the proceedings as televised from the courtroom. But the inquiry cannot end there. From the moment the trial judge announces that a case will be televised it become a *cause célèbre*. The whole community, including prospective jurors, becomes interested in all the morbid details surrounding it. The approaching trial immediately assumes an important status in the public press and the accused is highly publicized along with the offense with which he is charged. Every juror carries with him into the jury box these solemn facts and thus increases the chance of prejudice that is present

181

in every criminal case. . . . If the community be hostile to an accused a televised juror, realizing that he must return to neigh-
bors who saw the trial themselves, may well be led "not to hold
the balance nice, clear and true between the State and the accused."

Sheppard was accused of the murder of his wife in 1954.
The Supreme Court denied review of his conviction. Ten
years later an application for habeas corpus granted by a
lower federal court was set aside by the Court of Appeals.
The Supreme Court reinstated the lower-court decision because of the extent of the pretrial news coverage and the way
reporters in the courtroom caused confusion and interfered
with the defendant's ability to confer with his lawyer. Justice
Clark again wrote the opinion (384 U.S. 333, 1966) and said:

> From the cases coming here we note that unfair and prejudi-
> cial news comment on pending trials has become increasingly
> prevalent. Due process requires that the accused receive a trial
> by an impartial jury free from outside influences. Given the per-
> vasiveness of modern communications and the difficulty of
> effacing prejudicial publicity from the minds of the jurors, the
> trial courts must take strong measures to ensure that the bal-
> ance is never weighed against the accused. And appellate tribu-
> nals have the duty to make an independent evaluation of the
> circumstances. Of course, there is nothing that proscribes the
> press from reporting events that transpire in the courtroom.
> But where there is a reasonable likelihood that prejudicial news
> prior to trial will prevent a fair trial, the judge should continue
> the case until the threat abates, or transfer it to another county
> not so permeated with publicity. In addition, sequestration of
> the jury was something the judge should have raised *sua sponte*
> with counsel. If publicity during the proceedings threatens the
> fairness of the trial, a new trial should be ordered.

A curious variation of the publicity problem arose in the
case of the Reverend James E. Groppi, a Milwaukee civil
rights activist who was charged with resisting arrest, a mis-

demeanor under state law. He sought a change in the place of trial because of extensive unfavorable publicity. This was denied because under state law there could be no such change in a misdemeanor case. The Supreme Court ruled that he was thus denied the right to a trial by an impartial jury.

33. Trial by Jury

You are entitled to trial by jury in any case involving a serious penalty, and that jury must be fairly chosen.

You are not entitled to have a person of your own race or sex on the jury.

Nothing is more characteristic of Anglo-American jurisprudence than the jury system. Trial by a jury of one's "peers" was guaranteed by the Magna Carta. Originally the guarantee was intended to assure to nobles the right to be judged only by nobles, but it was one that proved valuable to ordinary people as well.

There are two provisions that deal with jury trials in criminal cases:

The trial of all crimes, except in cases of impeachment, shall be by jury; and such trial shall be held in the State where the said crimes shall have been committed; but when not committed within any State, the trial shall be at such place or places as the Congress may by law have directed. [Art. III, Sec. 2, cl. 3]

In all criminal prosecutions, the accused shall enjoy the right to a speedy and public trial by an impartial jury of the State and district wherein the crime shall have been committed, which district shall have been previously ascertained by law. [Sixth Amendment.]

The Seventh Amendment provides for jury trials in all federal civil cases involving more than twenty dollars. It has had no impact on freedom.

33a. *The Right to a Jury*

The guarantee of trial by jury has been applicable to the states, except at hearings in juvenile courts, since 1968, and controls all prosecutions where punishment might exceed six months. In 1970 the Court ruled that a six-man jury was permissible. In 1972 the Court upheld a state law which permitted convictions by a 9-3 vote in a non-capital case.

Congress has the right to eliminate trial by jury in the District of Columbia for petty offenses. It is probable that the six-month penalty rule would be applicable there also.

At one time the Court held that there was no right to trial by jury in contempt cases. The issue was presented by Governor Barnett of Mississippi when charged with obstruction of James Meredith's enrollment in the state university. Later the Court ruled there must be a jury if the punishment exceeds six months (see section 1d). The net effect of this ruling is that when a judge plans to charge a person with contempt he must make up his mind at the outset that the punishment will not be for more than six months if he wants to handle the case without a jury. In the case of the Chicago Seven, Judge Hoffman tried to circumvent this requirement by charging various of the defendants and lawyers with a number of separate acts and imposing six months imprisonment on each. The Appeals Court held that this was improper.

In 1969 the Court upheld a conviction for violation of an injunction obtained by the Securities and Exchange Commission where the judge put the defendant on probation for three years on the theory that this was a petty offense. But the Court said that for possible violation of the probation no more than six months imprisonment could be imposed.

The guarantee of trial by jury applies to aliens. Many years ago the Court held invalid an act of Congress which permitted deportation of aliens who were in this country illegally and subjected them to imprisonment prior to deportation without the safeguards of an ordinary trial.

Early in the century the Supreme Court ruled that certain constitutional guarantees, such as indictment by grand jury and trial by jury, need not be extended to our insular possessions but must be extended to a continental territory (as Alaska then was).

The Sixth Amendment also requires that the jury be "impartial." The Supreme Court has condemned the practice of calling up women talesmen only from a list furnished by a particular organization. Justice Murphy stressed the necessity of so choosing a jury that it should be "a cross section of the community."

The Court has held that no federal jury is properly constituted if wage earners are systematically excluded nor, at least in a district where women generally serve on juries, if women are excluded. A state statute was unanimously upheld which limited jury service to those women who had registered for it. A majority of the Court intimated that a state might exclude women from jury service altogether.

In some states, as in New York, the practice has existed of selecting special juries for so-called important cases. These are generally drawn from upper-middle-class neighborhoods and have been described as blue-ribbon juries. The propriety of this practice has been challenged, but without success. The Supreme Court ruled that no showing had been made of an intention to discriminate against any group of the community.

The right of government employees to sit as jurors in criminal cases in the District of Columbia has troubled the courts for some time, particularly in cases that in any way involved loyalty or security as a result of the loyalty program which had been instituted by President Truman. Where trial judges had permitted the questioning of government employees with regard to their possible bias because of that loyalty program, the convictions were upheld. The result was otherwise where such questioning had not been allowed.

In 1968 the Court held unconstitutional the provision of the federal kidnapping act which gave the jury the sole right to fix the penalty as death on the ground that this burdened a defendant's right to a jury trial.

In the same year the Court held that it was improper to exclude jurors in a case in which the death penalty might be imposed merely because they had expressed conscientious objections to capital punishment.

33b. *A Speedy Trial*

You are entitled to be brought to trial without unreasonable delay.

It will be noted that the Sixth Amendment guarantees a *speedy* trial. Since 1967, that provision has bound the states. There has been relatively little litigation on the subject. Prosecution after delay of six years was held too long. And a state could not justify unreasonable delay merely because the defendant was a federal prisoner during that period, since the federal authorities could have been required to make him available to the state.

But the right to a speedy trial is one of those more honored in the breach than in the observance. The law is well settled; its application very uncertain. The riots in New York City in the fall of 1970 brought to public attention the detention of thousands of persons awaiting trial in terribly crowded jails for periods of many months. More liberal bail practices, more money for judges, court and jail facilities, and public defenders are badly needed before these intolerable conditions will disappear.

34. The Right to Defend Oneself

While the right to defend oneself in court is inherent in every
civilized code of law, this privilege did not always include either the right to have a lawyer or the right to testify on one's
own behalf. In England, until comparatively recent times, a
defendant was considered so interested in the outcome of his
case as to be disqualified to act as a witness. Moreover, lawyers were not allowed to persons charged with serious crime
in the English courts until 1836. This denial of counsel had
been denounced by English statesmen and lawyers as early as
1758, and it was entirely rejected in the colonies. Various
state constitutions adopted during and immediately after the
Revolution established the right of anyone accused of crime
to be represented by a lawyer. When the federal Bill of
Rights was adopted, it followed the American rather than the
English practice:

> In all criminal prosecutions, the accused shall enjoy the right
> . . . to be informed of the nature and cause of the accusation; to
> be confronted with the witnesses against him; to have compul-
> sory process for obtaining witnesses in his favor, and to have
> the assistance of counsel for his defense. [Sixth Amendment]

The first part of this amendment covers what had already
been covered by the due process clause of the Fifth.

The Supreme Court has held that it is a denial of due process when a state judge refuses to issue a subpoena requested
by the defense for material witnesses.

34a. *Confrontation*

*You have the right to be present when witnesses testify
against you and to cross-examine them.*

*But if you disturb the proceedings the judge can proceed in
your absence.*

The extent of the right of confrontation was first passed on
by the Supreme Court in 1899. Then it held invalid an act of
Congress which permitted the conviction of a thief to be used
as proof that goods had been stolen in a prosecution against
their alleged receiver. Such a law, the Court ruled, denied the
defendant on trial of the right to cross-examine the witnesses
to the theft.

Until 1965 the Court had refused to apply this right of confrontation to state prosecutions. But in that year it ruled that
the right of confrontation cannot be denied by a state court,
and that it had been so denied when testimony taken at a preliminary hearing was used at the trial because the state had
made no effort to have the witness, then in a federal prison,
brought to the trial. It is also a violation of this guarantee to
refuse the demand of a defendant's lawyer that the chief witness for the prosecution state his correct name and his ad-
dress.

Problems have arisen with regard to the use of statements
by a codefendant who does not take the witness stand when
the statement implicates another defendant. In 1968 the
Court held that it was improper to allow such a statement because there was no opportunity to cross-examine the codefendant who had made it. But two years later, in a 5 to 4 decision the Court upheld a Georgia conviction under a state law
which permitted the use of such a statement. It is not clear
whether this represents a withdrawal from the earlier ruling
or is merely a recognition of the right of a state to set up its
own rules of evidence. The justices composing the majority
differed as to the reasons for upholding the convictions. Justice Stewart, joined by Chief Justice Burger and Justices
White and Blackmun, took the position that Georgia had the
right to prescribe a rule of evidence which permitted out-of-
court statements of conspirators to be used against any of
them so long as they were hiding their complicity. Justice
Harlan joined in upholding the conviction on the ground that
there was no real issue of confrontation, but one of due pro-

cess, and that the result, under all the circumstances, was a fair one. Justice Blackmun wrote a separate opinion concurred in by the Chief Justice on the ground that the other evidence against the accused man was so strong that the hearsay could be disregarded. In 1971 the use of such a statement was upheld where the codefendant had testified and denied having made the statement.

An interesting question arose in 1970 in the *Allen* case. There a state judge had excluded a defendant from the courtroom because of his persistent disruption of the trial. The Supreme Court upheld the judge's right to do so. Justice Black said (397 U.S. 337):

> It is not pleasant to hold that the respondent Allen was properly banished from the court for a part of his own trial. But our courts, palladiums of liberty as they are, cannot be treated disrespectfully with impunity. Nor can the accused be permitted by his disruptive conduct indefinitely to avoid being tried on the charges brought against him. It would degrade our country and our judicial system to permit our courts to be bullied, insulted, and humiliated and their orderly progress thwarted and obstructed by defendants brought before them charged with crimes. As guardians of the public welfare, our state and federal judicial systems strive to administer equal justice to the rich and the poor, the good and the bad, the native and foreign born of every race, nationality and religion. Being manned by humans, the courts are not perfect and are bound to make some errors. But, if our courts are to remain what the Founders intended, the citadels of justice, their proceedings cannot and must not be infected with the sort of scurrilous, abusive language and conduct paraded before the Illinois trial judge in this case. The record shows that the Illinois judge at all times conducted himself with that dignity, decorum, and patience that befit a judge.

In 1963 the Court ruled that a person could not be denied admission to the bar on the basis of unfavorable information without an opportunity to confront his accusers.

34b. *Counsel*

You are entitled to the advice of counsel at every meaningful stage of a prosecution.

Since the Sixth Amendment guarantees the right of all persons prosecuted in federal courts to representation by counsel, a denial of that right completely vitiates a federal conviction.

In dealing with state cases the Supreme Court until 1963 distinguished between a situation in which an accused was denied the right to consult a lawyer he had selected and one in which the court refused to appoint a lawyer when the accused was unable to procure one. In the former case a conviction could not stand; in the latter it depended on the circumstances. Where the offense was punishable by death the Supreme Court in effect presumed that denial of counsel would affect the accused's rights and reversed convictions. In other cases the Court considered the complexity of the charge and the experience and education of the accused to determine whether he had been harmed by the denial of counsel. If there was doubt about the circumstances the state court was required to hold a hearing.

In the *Gideon* case, in 1963, the Court unanimously repudiated the old doctrine and ruled that counsel must always be provided. And in 1967 the Court extended this requirement to juveniles.

The Court has ruled that failure to let an indicted person have a lawyer present at a lineup will result in reversal of conviction unless it can be shown that the identification at the trial had not been tainted by the lineup viewing. Where, as in some states, valuable rights may be lost if not asserted at the time of arraignment, a defendant is entitled to counsel at that time. Counsel must be provided in all cases where there is a possibility of a jail sentence.

The right to representation extends to the time of sentence

and also to a resentencing after revocation of probation. But failure to have a lawyer when pleading guilty has been held harmless because a lawyer was present at the time of sentence and could have moved to withdraw the plea of guilty. Where the right to appeal is dependent under state law on a showing of merit, an indigent convict is entitled to have counsel provided.

In *Miranda*, decided in 1966 chiefly on grounds of self-incrimination (see section 37), the Court laid down rules which forbade the use of statements taken from a person in custody in the absence of a lawyer unless he has been told of his right to have a lawyer provided for him.

The right to counsel may, however, be waived. Waiver may result from a plea of guilty, but not necessarily so. Mere failure to ask for a lawyer is not a waiver. And the Supreme Court held that an inexperienced, poorly educated seventeen-year-old who pleaded guilty to a charge of murder could not have intelligently waived his right, even though he said he didn't want a lawyer. If there is dispute about the facts the court must hold a hearing to determine whether there was a waiver.

As the first *Scottsboro* decision showed in 1932, it is not enough that an accused person be given a lawyer by the court. The lawyer must have a real chance to represent his client. Convictions of nine Negro boys accused of raping two white girls on a moving freight train were reversed in that case because the lawyers appointed by the state had no opportunity to investigate the facts of the crime and the defendants were hurried to trial in an atmosphere of hysteria.

An interesting problem arose in the *Groban* case. There a state law provided that a fire marshal might examine persons in secret and without counsel to determine the cause of any fire. The Court ruled that this violated no constitutional right since the proceeding was not directed against anyone and any witness might plead his privilege against self-incrimination.

Another question with regard to effective representation
by counsel came up in 1970. A defendant was represented by
a Legal Aid Society attorney in Pennsylvania at a trial at
which the jury disagreed. A different Legal Aid lawyer acted
for him at the second trial and saw him only a few minutes
before the trial began. No lawyer had communicated with the
defendant between the two trials. The Supreme Court found
no prejudice to the defendant. Justice Harlan disagreed.

35. Alibis

A common defense is that the accused was at some other
place at the time the crime was committed. Many states require a defendant to let the prosecution know in advance of
trial if he intends to put in such a defense and, if so, to give
details. Such laws are valid only if the state is required to let
the defendant know how it plans to meet his defense.

36. Guilty Pleas

A plea of guilty will be upheld if knowingly made.

Most criminal prosecutions are disposed of by the defendant's
plea of guilty. The Supreme Court has ruled that unless the
record shows that the defendant understood what he was
doing the plea cannot stand.

In many situations the defendant will plead guilty in the
hope of receiving a more lenient sentence. A dramatic instance of that was decided by the Supreme Court in 1970. A
man was charged with kidnapping in violation of federal law
which permitted a jury to impose the death penalty. Rather

than run that risk the defendant pleaded guilty and was sentenced to life imprisonment. The Supreme Court upheld that sentence. In another case the defendant, hoping to avoid the death penalty for first-degree murder, pleaded guilty but at the same time protested his innocence. The Supreme Court upheld his conviction because the trial court had heard evidence which implicated him in the crime before he had accepted the plea.

This practice of pleading guilty to avoid severe sentence often takes the form of a plea to an offense that carries a lesser punishment than the offense originally charged against the defendant. That practice is often called plea bargaining because it involves an agreement on the part of the prosecutor to accept the lesser plea. In theory, at least, the judge is not supposed to have taken any part in the process. It is his duty to make sure that the defendant understood what he was doing and had not been induced to do it by any threats or improper promises.

37. Self-Incrimination

The government cannot compel a person to incriminate himself unless it has given him immunity.

The notion that no one should be forced to incriminate himself goes back to English history. It was first formulated early in the seventeenth century when the Puritans opposed the methods used by the Stuarts in heresy prosecutions. One Lilburn resisted attempts to require him to answer questions about books he was charged with having written. In 1641 he induced the "Long Parliament" to abolish the practice of compelling suspected persons to give evidence. It may well be that the privilege was associated in the popular mind with the

presumption of innocence so unique in Anglo-American jurisprudence, a principle that has no constitutional expression.

Yet no part of the Constitution has been so widely criticized as this one since it enables the one person who might
know most about a crime to avoid having to tell what he
knows. This guarantee is contained in the Fifth Amendment:
"nor shall [any person] be compelled in any criminal case to
be a witness against himself."

While this language of the Fifth Amendment appears to be
rather limited it has, on the whole, received a liberal interpretation. Until 1964 this was not a restriction on state action.
But now no one can be compelled by any government agency
to answer incriminating questions or produce documents unless he is granted immunity.

In 1972 the Court upheld state and federal laws that did
not grant immunity from prosecution for any matter disclosed, but did bar the use of answers, or leads obtained from
them. The majority held that a person granted immunity and
compelled to answer incriminating questions was no worse off
than if he had not answered, since his answers, or leads from
them, could not be used against him. Justices Douglas and
Marshall dissented, believing that no one should be compelled
to answer unless given immunity from prosecution—transaction immunity. Brennan and Rehnquist abstained.

The privilege against self-incrimination has been claimed,
not always with success, in a number of situations where actually no spoken words were called for. The Supreme Court
has held that it is not a violation of the privilege to compel a
suspect to give a specimen of his handwriting, to wear certain
clothes in a lineup, or to allow blood to be taken in order to
determine whether the suspect had been drunk when driving.
So there is no violation of the privilege when a state law requires a person charged with crime to let the prosecution
know that he intends to plead an alibi—that is, to show that
he was at some place other than the place of the crime—and
to disclose the details of the alibi. But it is a violation of the

privilege for a prosecutor to comment on the failure of a defendant to testify. The privilege is not violated by a law which requires the driver of an automobile involved in an accident to identify himself. And when a person is required to file a report that might indicate that he was violating some law he can claim his privilege; otherwise he cannot. Thus a person cannot refuse to file an income tax return. But he can refuse to report that he is a gambler or a possessor of drugs or, in some places, of firearms, since such activities are generally prohibited. The Court in 1971 unanimously upheld an Act of Congress which made it a crime to possess sawed-off shotguns and similar weapons that were not registered because the law did not impose the obligation to register on the possessor but on the importer or manufacturer.

The privilege may be claimed in any proceeding, whether in a court, or before an administrative agency or a congressional or legislative committee. But the privilege is personal. A person cannot use it, therefore, to shield anyone else. And it cannot be claimed by an individual who is being questioned about his activities as an officer of an entity such as a corporation or labor union.

In the famous *Miranda* case (384 U.S. 436) the Supreme Court ruled in 1966 that once a person is in custody nothing he says can be used against him unless he has been told that he need not talk and that he has the right to have the advice of a lawyer.

Of course a person cannot refuse to answer every question put to him by invoking his privilege. There must be something in the nature of the question or the surrounding circumstances that justifies an inference that a particular answer to the question might be directly incriminating or bring out information that might lead to incriminating matter. Ultimately, of course, the courts decide whether a claim of privilege was justified in the particular instance. But it is important to keep in mind that the person being questioned need not explain why he fears incrimination because to compel him to do that might well result in his incriminating himself.

The formula to be used is very simply: "I refuse to answer because to do so might tend to incriminate me." It is even enough simply to say: "I claim my privilege against self-incrimination," or "I rely on the Fifth Amendment."

The mere claim of the privilege has often had serious consequences, however. During the McCarthy investigations of the fifties, people who used the privilege to avoid answering questions about Communist affiliations were called Fifth Amendment Communists. Many persons lost their jobs, others were blacklisted. The Supreme Court set its face against the dismissal of persons from public employment or the disbarment of lawyers automatically because the privilege had been relied on. But where employees refused to answer questions put by their employers that were relevant to their employment, their dismissals were upheld.

In two 5 to 4 decisions the Court in 1958 sustained dismissals of state employees who had refused to answer questions with regard to Communist activities. Chief Justice Warren and Justices Black, Douglas, and Brennan dissented in each case.

In the *Beilan* case a schoolteacher had refused to answer questions put by his superintendent. More than a year later he claimed his privilege when questioned by the House Un-American Activities Committee. A week later charges of incompetence were preferred against him and he was dismissed. The Pennsylvania state court upheld the dismissal as justified by the refusal to answer questions put by the superintendent. A majority of the Supreme Court refused to look behind that reason.

In the *Lerner* case a subway conductor was dismissed under the New York State Security Risk Law because he refused to answer questions about Communist membership. A majority of the Supreme Court upheld this on the theory that there had been no finding of disloyalty, only one of unreliability, and that refusal to answer pertinent questions justified such finding.

The dissenters criticized both decisions as unrealistic—the first as failing to give weight to the fact that no proceedings were instituted until after the plea of the privilege before the House Un-American Activities Committee, the second as ignoring the actual effect of a security dismissal.

The Court in 1968 ruled that public employees could not be dismissed for refusing to waive the privilege against self-incrimination as required by local law. In 1973 that principle was applied to the case of a public contractor threatened with contract forfeiture and future disqualification.

Use of the privilege has often led to the assumption that it is, in effect, a confession of guilt. If a person has nothing to hide, it is said, why should he not answer questions. That attitude ignores the real reason for the privilege. As was said by Justice Field as long ago as 1894 (149 U.S. 60):

> It is not every one who can safely venture on the witness stand though entirely innocent of the charge against him. Excessive timidity, nervousness when facing others and attempting to explain transactions of a suspicious character, and offences charged against him, will often confuse and embarrass him to such a degree as to increase rather than remove prejudices against him. It is not every one, however honest, who would, therefore, willingly be placed on the witness stand.

And in 1908 Justice Moody described the privilege "as a privilege of great value, a protection to the innocent though a shelter to the guilty, and a safeguard against heedless, unfounded or tyrannical prosecutions" (211 U.S. 78).

Justice Clark reiterated those views in the *Slochower* case (350 U.S. 551, 1956):

> At the outset we must condemn the practice of imputing a sinister meaning to the exercise of a person's constitutional

right under the Fifth Amendment. The right of an accused person to refuse to testify, which had been in England merely a rule of evidence, was so important to our forefathers that they raised it to the dignity of a constitutional enactment, and it has been recognized as "one of the most valuable prerogatives of the citizen."

. . . The privilege against self-incrimination would be reduced to a hollow mockery if its exercise could be taken as equivalent either to a confession of guilt or a conclusive presumption of perjury. As we have pointed out in *Ullmann*, a witness may have a reasonable fear of prosecution and yet be innocent of any wrongdoing. The privilege serves to protect the innocent who otherwise might be ensnared by ambiguous circumstance. See Griswold, *The Fifth Amendment Today* (1955).

Like most constitutional guarantees this one can be waived. To what extent such waiver arises because of answers previously given is not altogether clear. The privilege should, therefore, be claimed very early in the questioning.

An interesting instance of the waiver problem occurred in 1951. A woman was called before a federal grand jury investigating possible violations of the Smith Act. She admitted that she was the treasurer of the local Communist party and had at one time been in possession of its records. But she refused to identify the person to whom she had turned these over. A majority of the Supreme Court ruled that she had waived any right to plead her privilege because she had admitted her Communist connections. Chief Justice Vinson said (340 U.S. 367):

where criminating facts have been voluntarily revealed, the privilege cannot be invoked to avoid disclosure of the details.

Justice Black dissented, with the concurrence of Justices Frankfurter and Douglas. He said:

Moreover, today's holding creates this dilemma for witnesses: On the one hand, they risk imprisonment for contempt by asserting the privilege prematurely; on the other, they might lose the privilege if they answer a single question. The Court's view makes the protection depend on timing so refined that lawyers, let alone laymen, will have difficulty in knowing when to claim it.

38. Presumptions

Laws which create presumptions of facts not proved are valid only if the presumptions have a reasonable basis.

Statutes which create presumptions are bad unless there is a reasonable connection between the fact established and the fact to be presumed. Thus a federal law was held unconstitutional which permitted an inference that the possessor of a gun knew that it had been illegally transported in interstate commerce merely because he had previously been convicted of a crime of violence.

In two cases the Court dealt with identical presumption provisions about persons found at an illegal still. In the first it upheld the conviction because the charge was only aiding and abetting. It reversed the conviction in the second because the charge there was possession and control. It distinguished the first case on the ground that presence might indicate participation in operation but not control.

In 1969 the Court unanimously held that there was no rational basis for the presumption that a possessor of marijuana knew it had been illegally imported because so much of that plant is of domestic growth. This rule was extended in the following year to cocaine because coca leaves can be legally imported for medical purposes. But the Court held the rule not applicable to heroin because opium poppy capsules from which it is derived cannot be legally imported.

39. Perjured Testimony

*The government cannot use testimony of a witness it knew
was committing perjury.*

In 1916 a bomb exploded in San Francisco during a Prepared-
ness Day parade, killing some people. Tom Mooney and Warren K. Billings, two radical labor leaders, were convicted and
sentenced to death. The intervention of President Wilson
based on strong doubts about the case expressed by our Allies
in the war resulted in commutation to life imprisonment. Agi-
tation continued for years. Finally, in a habeas corpus proceeding brought by Mooney the contention was made that his
conviction rested on testimony which the prosecution knew
was false. The Supreme Court ruled that this contention required a hearing at which its truth or falsity could be established, for the first time laying down the principle that the deliberate use of perjured testimony by a prosecutor was a
denial of due process and was therefore prohibited by the
Fourteenth Amendment. The Court, however, compelled
Mooney to seek redress in the courts of California. And when
those courts ruled that there had been no knowing use of perjured testimony the Supreme Court refused to interfere.
However, both Mooney and Billings were later freed by Governor Olson.

In a later case the Court unanimously ruled that a state
conviction was invalid because the prosecutor had claimed
that a pair of shorts belonging to the defendant had blood
stains on them when he knew that the stains had been made
by red paint.

The principle of these cases has been applied to cases where
the prosecution has kept from the defense information which
was favorable to it.

40. Husbands and Wives

Except in limited situations one spouse may not testify against another.

The marriage relationship has had some curious legal aspects. Until comparatively modern times a married woman was subject to her husband in most respects relating to property. There was a fiction that they were legally one person which, like most fictions, had only partial validity. While it lasted neither husband nor wife could testify either for or against the other except where the wife claimed that the husband had committed an offense against her person.

The ban on a person's testifying *for* a spouse rested on the fiction of identity and on the rule, long abolished, that a defendant could not testify in his own behalf because of the strong temptation to testify falsely. The ban on a person's testifying *against* a spouse rested on a desire to foster peace in the family. The Supreme Court, in 1933, rejected the first of these bans. When the second part of the ban came before the Court in 1958 it adhered to the old rule. The case arose under the Mann Act. The defendant's wife was allowed to testify at the trial that her husband had transported a girl across state lines for immoral purposes. The Supreme Court unanimously ruled that such testimony was improper. Justice Black said (358 U.S. 74):

> While the rule forbidding testimony of one spouse *for* the other was supported by reasons which time and changing legal practices had undermined, we are not prepared to say the same about the rule barring testimony of one spouse *against* the other. The basic reason that the law has refused to pit wife against husband or husband against wife in a trial where life or liberty is at stake was a belief that such a policy is necessary to foster family peace, not only for the benefit of husband, wife,

and children, but for the benefit of the public as well. Such a belief has never been unreasonable and is not now. Moreover, it is
difficult to see how family harmony is less disturbed by a wife's
voluntary testimony against her husband than by her compelled
testimony. In truth, it seems probable that much more bitter-
ness would be engendered by voluntary testimony than by that
which is compelled. The Government argues that the fact a husband or wife testifies against the other voluntarily is strong indication that the marriage is already gone. Doubtless this is
often true. But not all marital flare-ups in which one spouse
wants to hurt the other are permanent. The widespread success
achieved by courts throughout the country in conciliating family differences is a real indication that some apparently broken
homes can be saved provided no unforgivable act is done by either party. Adverse testimony given in criminal proceedings
would, we think, be likely to destroy almost any marriage.

Two years later the Court was confronted with the excep-
tion—the case of an offense committed against the wife. Only
there the woman had not been the wife when the offense, violation of the Mann Act, was committed. The Court approved
the use of the wife's testimony even though the wife had
objected to testifying. In so doing Justice Brennan pointed
out that the purpose of the Mann Act was to protect weak
women from bad men. He was careful to limit the rule announced to Mann Act prosecutions. Chief Justice Warren and
Justices Black and Douglas dissented. They rejected the majority's assumption that the man might have "mesmerized"
the woman.

Congress has expressly permitted spouses to testify against
each other in certain situations, providing in some that such
testimony could not be compelled. State laws on the subject
vary greatly and should be consulted when problems in the
area arise.

A different aspect of the husband-wife relationship was involved in another case decided in 1960. The government indicted a married couple for conspiracy to bring merchandise

into the United States illegally with intent to defraud the government. The lower federal court dismissed the indictment on the ground that husband and wife were legally incapable of conspiring with each other. The Supreme Court reversed this decision. Justice Frankfurter rejected the ancient fiction of legal identity which he said had been respected "parrot-like." He said (364 U.S. 51):

> For this Court now to act on Hawkins's formulation of the medieval view that husband and wife "are esteemed but as one Person in Law, and are presumed to have but one Will" would indeed be "blind imitation of the past." It would require us to disregard the vast changes in the status of women—the extension of her rights and correlative duties—whereby a wife's legal submission to her husband has been wholly wiped out, not only in the English-speaking world generally but emphatically so in this country.

Chief Justice Warren and Justices Black and Whittaker dissented. They did not base their dissent on the fiction of identity but, as the Chief Justice said:

> A wife, simply by virtue of the intimate life she shares with her husband, might easily perform acts that would technically be sufficient to involve her in a criminal conspiracy with him, but which might be far removed from the arm's-length agreement typical of that crime. It is not a medieval mental quirk or an attitude "unnourished by sense" to believe that husbands and wives should not be subjected to such a risk, or that such a possibility should not be permitted to endanger the confidentiality of the marriage relationship.

It should be noted that these decisions rested on the Supreme Court's supervisory power over federal courts and not on any constitutional basis. It is doubtful, therefore, whether the Supreme Court would act where a state criminal court allowed one spouse to testify against another.

41. Statements by Witnesses

*You are entitled to see statements made to the prosecution
by witnesses called by it at your trial.*

It is often vitally important to a defense lawyer to know if a
prosecution witness is succumbing to the quite prevalent, perhaps unconscious, habit of embroidering or exaggerating. All
too many people feel, when on the witness stand, that they
must never admit ignorance. The best way to check on an
overwilling witness is to compare his statements in court with
what he may have said on some earlier occasion, as to a grand
jury, or just to the prosecutor. The natural demand of the defense lawyer to see such earlier statements is usually resisted
by the prosecutor. The practice developed of having the judge
look at the earlier statements to see if they contained inconsistencies with the trial testimony.

Naturally that did not satisfy defense lawyers. One enter-
prising lawyer took his case to the Supreme Court and won.
The Court ruled that the lawyer must have the right to determine for himself whether or not the earlier material showed
inconsistencies. From the name of the lawyer's client this became known as the *Jencks* rule. One of the grounds of prosecution objection to inspection by the defense was that there
might be matter in the earlier statement affecting the security of the government. Such an objection, said the Court,
gave the government the choice of dropping the prosecution
or letting the material be seen. So far this rule has not been
applied to state prosecutions.

The *Jencks* decision aroused controversy, and a few months
later (September 1957) Congress passed a law which somewhat limited its scope. The Court, in upholding the law, ruled
that notes taken by an agent need not be made available to
the defense except where the witness had adopted the notes.
And in a later case the Court held that testimony given by a

witness before a grand jury need not be shown the defense
unless a real necessity was shown.

42. Contempt of Court

*A judge may punish disruptive conduct in the court room or
refusal to answer a proper question.*

*A judge may not impose punishment for more than six
months unless there has been a trial by jury.*

When a disruptive act occurs in open court the judge may
punish the offender for contempt without holding a hearing.
But he may not do this when the offense has not been committed before him. Refusal to answer a question before a
grand jury is not an affront to the dignity of the Court and so
cannot be summarily punished. To punish such a contempt
the offender must be given notice of the charge against him
and an opportunity to defend himself. But refusal to answer a
proper question in open court can be punished without a hearing.

Problems sometimes arise about the propriety of permitting the judge who has been offended to impose the punishment. This problem arose when Judge Medina punished several of the lawyers who had acted for the leaders of the
Communist party in a prosecution under the Smith Act for
conspiracy to advocate the overthrow of the government by
force. At the end of the long trial the judge read a detailed
statement of the various acts of the lawyers he considered to
have been contemptuous and at once found them guilty. He
imposed varying terms of imprisonment. The Supreme Court
upheld these convictions, largely on the ground that the lawyers had been repeatedly warned. Their argument that the
judge had no right to wait until the end of the trial was re-

jected on the ground that for the judge to have found them
guilty each time an improper act occurred might have prejudiced the case of their clients. But many years later the Court
reversed a summary conviction for contempt because the
judge had become so personally embroiled with the lawyer
that he no longer represented the "impersonal authority of
the law."

Finally in 1971 the Court ruled that a judge ordinarily may
not wait until the end of a trial to find a defendant guilty of
contempt. If he does wait the contempt charge must be tried
before a different judge and the defendant must be given a
hearing.

Problems have arisen where the alleged contempt consisted
of the violation of an order ultimately held to have been
improperly made. The Supreme Court has upheld the convictions unless the court which made the order lacked jurisdiction or no practical review of the order was possible before
the prohibited event. However, in some instances the contempt convictions were sent back to the original court for
reconsideration in the light of the finding of invalidity, and
occasionally convictions have been set aside.

A defendant who refused to answer eleven questions about
the Communist connections of other people was convicted on
eleven counts. That, said the Supreme Court, was improper,
since all the questions dealt with the same subject.

(For related issues in contempt see also section 1d.)

43. Cruel and Unusual Punishment

The prohibition of the Eighth Amendment against punishment that is "cruel and unusual" was designed primarily to
prevent maiming and other bodily indignities. The Supreme
Court held that electrocution was not such an indignity. And
a majority of the Court ruled that it did not constitute cruel

and unusual punishment to subject a man to the ordeal of a second electrocution after the first attempt had failed because of a mechanical defect.

But the Court struck down a Philippine law because it prescribed a much more severe punishment for a minor offense than for much more serious offenses.

An interesting application of the principle arose in the *Trop* case in 1958. A native-born citizen who applied for a passport so that he could work for an airplane company abroad was told by the State Department that he had lost his American citizenship under a law passed during the Civil War because he had been convicted by court-martial of desertion in wartime. The majority of the Supreme Court held that the law which required this result had been beyond the power of Congress to pass (see section 13). Four of the justices held also that such a taking away of American citizenship was cruel and unusual punishment because it left the man stateless.

A few years later the Court held that a California law inflicted cruel and unusual punishment when it imposed punishment for drug addiction. But the Court refused to hold that a law which punished a person for being drunkenly incapacitated in public constituted such punishment. Justice Marshall said (392 U.S. 514, 1968):

> On its face the present case does not fall within that holding, since appellant was convicted, not for being a chronic alcoholic, but for being in public while drunk on a particular occasion. The State of Texas thus has not sought to punish a mere status, as California did in *Robinson*; nor has it attempted to regulate appellant's behavior in the privacy of his own home. Rather, it has imposed upon appellant a criminal sanction for public behavior which may create substantial health and safety hazards, both for appellant and for members of the general public, and which offends the moral and esthetic sensibilities of a large segment of the community. This seems a far cry from convicting one for being an addict, being a chronic alcoholic, being "mentally ill or a leper".

Imposition of the death penalty for rape when the victim had not otherwise been injured has been challenged in recent years, generally without success. In June 1972 the Court ruled that capital punishment as practiced in most of the states was unconstitutional. The four Nixon appointees dissented.

44. Post-Trial Matters

In a decision with far-reaching implications the Court ruled that a convict who had been found insane while serving a sentence could not be detained in prison after the expiration of his sentence and was entitled to the benefit of the procedures available to persons civilly committed; otherwise he was denied equal protection of the laws.

In the *Griffin* case the Court held that a state's refusal to provide an indigent prisoner with a free transcript for purposes of appeal was a denial of equal protection. This principle was applied in 1958 to a Washington conviction where the point was raised more than twenty years after the conviction. But in a case where the transcript had become unavailable after a long lapse of time and the prisoner's lawyer had made no attempt to get it while it was still available, the conviction was not disturbed.

A Washington law required that an indigent could obtain a transcript for appeal only if the trial judge certified that the appeal was not frivolous. The Supreme Court struck this law down because any claim of error could properly be considered only after an examination of some part of the transcript. An Indiana law permitting the furnishing of a transcript to an indigent only at the request of the Public Defender was held invalid.

The Court held invalid a Pennsylvania law which allowed a jury to determine whether the defendant, though acquitted, should pay the trial costs, on the ground that the law set up no standards for the guidance of juries in making their determination.

45. Double Jeopardy

The government cannot try a person twice for the same offense.

But there is considerable uncertainty about whether crimes affecting several persons constitute one or several offenses.

Protection against double jeopardy is one of the guarantees that had no specific connection with English history. It is of very ancient origin, having existed in the law of the European continent, the so-called civil law, which was derived from Roman law. It stems from the belief that when a matter has once been litigated the decision should be final. It is similar to the rule applicable to ordinary law suits and known to lawyers as *res adjudicata.* The guarantee is found in the Fifth Amendment:

nor shall any person be subject for the same offense to be twice put in jeopardy of life or limb.

Like so many constitutional guarantees this one requires explanation. It is not confined to the "life or limb" of the text, but is a guarantee against double prosecution for the same offense. However, it is difficult to determine when it applies.

If a person convicted of crime appeals and the court orders a new trial, the constitutional provision has no application at all. And that makes sense, as the convicted person had taken the step that produced the second trial. But at this second trial he cannot be convicted of a greater offense than he had been at the first. So if a person is prosecuted for murder and the jury brings in a verdict of murder in the second degree, the new trial cannot result in a verdict of first-degree murder. In a case in which a defendant was charged with murder but the jury brought in a verdict of manslaughter, the Supreme Court held it improper afterward to try him again on the murder charge even though, at the second trial, the jury again found only manslaughter. Nor can there be more severe punishment, unless this is justified by new information, and if so this must be set out in the record. If a conviction is set aside on appeal and the defendant is again convicted, any time he served on the first sentence must be credited on the second.

There are other situations in which a second trial is permissible, as where the first became abortive through no fault of the prosecution. The Supreme Court upheld a new trial in one case where the first one was ended because it appeared that one of the jurors was disqualified and in another where the judge stopped the first because he believed that the prosecutor had prejudiced the defense by overstepping the bounds of propriety. But the Court held it improper to hold a second trial where the first was ended because of the absence of a key prosecution witness, or when a judge ends the first trial because he believes that some of the prosecution witnesses have not been adequately warned that they might be incriminating themselves by their testimony. In the latter case, decided in 1971, Justices Stewart, White, and Blackmun dissented.

The question of what constitutes the same offense has troubled the Court. In two cases it permitted the trial of a person charged with holding up one member of a group after he had been acquitted at an earlier trial for holding up others in the same group, even though it appeared that the acquittal rested on doubt about the identity of the accused. But the Court indicated that this would be improper if the second prosecution savored of persecution. A different result was reached some years later under substantially the same circumstances. In the later case Justice Brennan said that "all the charges against a defendant which grow out of a single criminal act, occurrence, episode or transaction" should be tried together.

Since 1969 this guarantee has bound the states and prevents prosecution for the same offense by a state and also one of its subdivisions. When an offense is a violation of both state and federal law, prosecution by both authorities despite an acquittal in one jurisdiction is not a violation of the guarantee unless it appears that the authorities in the jurisdiction in which there had been the acquittal brought pressure on the authorities of the other to start a prosecution.

46. Convicts' Rights

Aside from trying to get out of jail on the ground that they had been denied some constitutional right at their trial, many convicts have asked the courts to remedy prison conditions. Their complaints cover a wide field. The Black Muslims want religious facilities and object to a diet which violates their scruples. There are complaints against excessive punishment for minor violations of prison rules, against racial discrimination and segregation, against censorship of reading matter and mail, against lack of access to lawyers.

In every jail there are convicts who have studied the opinions of the Supreme Court and help others to frame habeas corpus petitions. The Supreme Court held it improper for prison authorities to forbid this and to discipline a convict who violated such a rule.

In February 1971 the United States Court of Appeals that sits in New York upheld a judgment for $13,000 which a convict had obtained against New York's Commissioner of Correction and the warden of the prison. He had been kept in solitary confinement because he had been defiant, had refused to answer questions, and had assisted other convicts with legal papers. The Court rejected the view expressed by the lower federal court that this constituted "cruel and unusual punishment" (see section 43) but agreed that the punishment was unjustified. The Court laid down guidelines for the protection of the rights of convicts: prison officials have no right to censor mail sent by a convict to any court, public agency, or lawyer with regard to his conviction or complaints he wanted to make about his treatment in prison. The Court also indicated that prisoners were entitled to safeguards of a substantial nature against arbitrary discipline. These safeguards include notice of the grounds for the discipline, an opportunity to reply, and a reasonable investigation.

47. Miscellaneous Questions in Criminal Cases

It is elementary that a person is entitled to be informed of the charges against him. That rule was applied in 1968 to a state disbarment proceeding.

It is also "sheer denial" of due process to convict a person for a crime with which he was not charged or if there is no evidence of the crime charged. Thus a Louisville conviction for disorderly conduct resulting in a fine of ten dollars was set aside on a direct appeal to the Supreme Court because of total absence of proof of the offense charged. When a segregationist group was convicted of contempt in violation of an injunction against holding a meeting, the Court reversed the conviction in 1963 on the ground there was no evidence that the injunction had been violated.

In 1966 the Court ruled that a juvenile was entitled to certain due process safeguards, particularly to a hearing with representation by counsel, before the Juvenile Court could order him tried in an ordinary criminal court. And in 1967 in the *Gault* case this rule was extended to afford juveniles all due process requirements at all stages.

Colorado has a Sex Offender Act under which a person convicted of a specific sex offense may be given an indeterminate sentence without a hearing after a psychiatric examination. This the Court held was a denial of due process.

A Texas law was upheld which allowed a jury to find that a defendant should be sentenced as a habitual criminal at a trial for a specific offense. There the jury was allowed to hear of earlier convictions in connection with the issue of sentence but was instructed that it could not consider these on the issue of guilt.

The Court held it a denial of due process to refuse a defendant subpoenas he requested for material witnesses. It unanimously rejected a contention that a state lost the right to try a person accused of crime even if he was forcibly taken into the state in violation of the federal kidnapping law.

The Court ruled that a person could not be charged with violation of an ordinance requiring convicts to register if he had no knowledge of the existence of the ordinance.

In *Raley* v. *Ohio* the Court held due process had been denied where witnesses who had pleaded their privilege against self-incrimination were later punished for contempt on the ground that state law granted immunity when, in fact, the tribunal before whom they appeared had assumed that the witnesses had the right to rely on their privilege.

The Court reversed a murder conviction where vital testimony was given by two deputy sheriffs who, during the trial, were in charge of the jury. The Court held that a state conviction could not stand where, while the jury was deliberating, at least three jurors heard a bailiff express the opinion that the defendant was guilty.

In the *Rochin* case the Court unanimously reversed a con-

viction obtained by using a stomach pump to recover drugs
which the suspect had swallowed. But it refused to apply that
precedent to the *Irvine* case where the police had illegally entered an apartment and installed a microphone, although the
conduct of the police was excoriated. Later the Court held it
permissible to take blood from an unconscious man to determine whether he had been driving under the influence of liquor.

In 1969 the Court unanimously reversed a conviction based
on a guilty plea where the judge had not, as the federal rules
required, personally questioned the defendant about his understanding of the nature of the charge against him. The
same rule was later applied to a state case.

In the *Nugent* case a majority of the Court ruled that a
conviction for draft evasion was proper despite the contention by the registrant that he had been denied a fair hearing
on his claim to be exempted as a conscientious objector because he had been denied an opportunity to examine an FBI
report.

A conviction was set aside because the jurors had been allowed to read about earlier convictions of the defendant.

It is also a denial of due process for an appellate court to
sustain a conviction on a theory that had not been presented
to the jury at the trial. In such a situation a new trial should
be held.

48. Due Process in Civil Proceedings

Students who have been disciplined, teachers who have not
been reappointed, persons confined in institutions because it
is claimed that they are narcotics addicts or insane, and welfare recipients have with growing frequency asked the courts
to come to their assistance, claiming that their rights to due

process have been denied. While the general rule is well established that persons whose legal rights might be affected are entitled to notice of the proceeding and an opportunity to be heard, the Supreme Court has had few occasions to deal with these noncriminal situations.

In 1962 the Court dealt with the kind of notice that a municipality must give before exercising its right of condemnation. The city of New York wanted to divert the water of a river and gave notice to the owners of the lands bordering the river by putting posters on trees along the way and publishing in the City Record. The Supreme Court said this was insufficient notice and required notice by mail where the city knew the addresses of the owners.

In 1970 the Court ruled that welfare recipients were entitled to a hearing before benefits could be taken from them.

In 1971 the Supreme Court upheld a lower federal court decision that a tenant in a federally assisted housing project was entitled to a hearing and representation by counsel before being evicted.

In 1971 the Court unanimously struck down a law that forfeited a driver's license after involvement in an accident because he was uninsured. The Court ruled there must be a hearing to determine if he was in any way at fault.

Problems have arisen in connection with the garnishment of wages on the commencement of a suit. In some states this may be done only if the debtor is a nonresident; in others it can be done even if the debtor is a resident. Some states allow the debtor an opportunity to challenge the attachment on technical grounds; others do not. In 1969 the Supreme Court held unconstitutional as a denial of due process a Wisconsin law which permitted the attachment of a resident's wages and gave him no opportunity to do anything about it until there had been a trial of the case. Later the Court held it improper to attach property, or seize it for default in payment, without notice and an opportunity to contest.

Procedures in
Vindicating Rights

What steps a person must take to ensure that his constitutional rights will be considered by the courts and ultimately by the United States Supreme Court may depend on whether the challenged infringement was caused by state agencies or by federal ones. His right to have the subject considered at all will depend on how directly it affects him. His rights may have been lost because the controversy has ended, that is, because moot. On the other hand, he may be able to assert rights once unavailable because of later decisions by the Supreme Court.

49. State Infringements

Where a state has started criminal proceedings the defendant should assert any rights he believes he has under the United

States Constitution as early and as often as possible. Unless he clearly raises a federal issue and continues to raise it in the highest court of the state to which he can go, he will be unable to get to the United States Supreme Court. (See page 7 for a particularly dramatic instance of such failure for omitting to press the federal issue in the state's highest court.)

If, on the other hand, a suit is commenced to vindicate a right claimed to have been infringed by some agency of the state, the first question to be considered is whether to bring the suit in a state or a federal court. Except in a few situations the right to sue in a federal court is restricted by law to cases in which the amount involved exceeds $10,000. This is called the "jurisdictional" amount. The theory of this limitation is that it will relieve the federal courts of the need to deal with cases of minor importance and leave these to the state courts. In some parts of the country, however, state courts have shown themselves to be hostile to certain kinds of claims. This question is becoming increasingly important on account of the number and variety of demonstrations and the repressive tactics often shown by local police and National Guard in the name of law and order. Fortunately Congress has exempted suits under the various civil rights acts from this monetary restriction.

When a suit is brought in a federal court challenging the constitutionality of a state statute which could be interpreted in such a way as to eliminate the defect, the federal court will ordinarily wait until the highest court of the state has interpreted the statute. But the federal court will keep its case alive until the state courts have acted. When there is no room for interpretation and only a federal constitutional issue is involved the federal court will decide it.

The Justices of the Supreme Court, however, are not always in agreement as to when a federal court should take on the issue of constitutionality or when it should wait for action by the highest court of the state. Early in 1971 this problem arose in connection with a Wisconsin law which permitted the listing in bars of persons thought to be alcoholics. The majority of the Court struck this law down on the ground that no hearing was provided. Chief Justice Burger and Justices Black and Blackmun thought the federal court should have "abstained" to give the state court the chance of passing on the question. Justice Douglas for the majority said the issue was so clear that there was no need for leaving this to the state courts.

When a state law impinges on freedom of expression, and waiting for state interpretation would result in extensive litigation because of the many aspects of the problem raised by the state statute and might have a "chilling" effect on freedom of expression, the federal courts should decide the basic constitutional issue without waiting for state courts' interpretation.

Where a case is brought in a state court the federal issue cannot be taken to the United States Supreme Court until an attempt has been made to take the case to the highest court of the state and the case has been finally decided. The Supreme Court recently relaxed the latter part of this requirement. Alabama prosecuted the editor of a newspaper for having written and published an editorial on election day urging the people to vote in a particular way. This was charged as a violation of a law which made it an offense to do any "electioneering" on the day of the election. The editor claimed that his right to free expression was violated. The state supreme court rejected that contention but sent the case back for trial. The United States Supreme Court denied an application by the state to dismiss the appeal made on the contention that the decision by the Alabama Supreme Court was not final. The Court recognized that this contention was formally true, but practically not. For, under the state court's ruling upholding the statute, the editor had no defense. Realities required disposition of the constitutional issue now. So the Supreme Court went on to hold the state law unconstitutional.

In a group of six cases decided in February 1971, the Su-

preme Court placed restrictions on the right of a federal statutory court to interfere with the enforcement of state criminal laws. There were 17 opinions in all; the principal ones
written by Justice Black. The Court was unanimous in ruling
that persons who have not been threatened with prosecution
have no right to sue to prevent enforcement of laws they believe to be unconstitutional. Over the sole dissent of Justice
Douglas, the Court decided that state prosecutions could not
be challenged in these three-judge statutory courts unless
there was "great and immediate" danger of injury to freedom, or the state authorities were using the challenged laws
in bad faith or to harass. Justice Black said that it was not
enough that a state law might possibly be unconstitutional
"on its face."

The press reported these rulings as curtailment of the role
of the three-judge courts. There is little doubt that these
courts will now be reluctant to entertain suits which challenge prosecutions under state laws. Except in unusual cases,
persons charged with violating state laws that they believe to
be unconstitutional will have to stand trial in the state courts.
Then, if their claims of violation of their constitutional rights
are rejected in all the state courts to which they can carry
their case, they will have to try to get their contentions considered by the United States Supreme Court. The process will
be lengthy and expensive, but there seems to be no alterna-
tive under these latest rulings. It remains to be seen whether
persons merely threatened with prosecution but who are not
actually being prosecuted can ask a statutory court to pass on
the constitutionality of the statute under which the threat is
made.

Two of the cases decided by the Supreme Court involved
prosecutions under state criminal anarchy laws (see Section
1a), one from California, the other, involving Black Panthers,
from New York. Justice Douglas dissented in the first of
these cases because the defendant in the state prosecution
had been charged only with speech; he did not dissent in the

second because the charge there included the possession of
weapons and the storing of gasoline for the purpose of setting
fires.

In another case several Negroes sued to enjoin their prosecution under various Illinois statutes on the ground that they
had been arrested during peaceful demonstrations without
probable cause and that their First Amendment rights had
been violated. The three-judge court had found only one of
the challenged laws to be unconstitutional and enjoined its
enforcement. The Supreme Court, Justice Douglas again dissenting, set this aside on the ground that no prosecution had
been threatened or begun under that particular law.

The remaining three cases involved various charges of obscenity. One, from Boston, challenged the banning of the motion picture, *I Am Curious (Yellow)*; another challenged the
seizure of material from a newspaper office in the night time,
an act which, in effect, closed down the paper; the third also
involved a search, challenged on the ground that there had
been no adversary hearing before the seizure. The Supreme
Court set aside all three statutory court decisions and ruled in
the last two cases that such a court had no power to deal with
the issue of unlawful seizure. Justice Douglas dissented from
that ruling. He did not participate in the Boston case.

A subsidiary question arose in the last of these cases. The
three-judge court rejected an attack made there on the constitutionality of various Louisiana obscenity laws, but upheld
such attack on an ordinance enacted by one of its parishes.
The Supreme Court ruled, in line with old precedent, that a
three-judge court had no authority to pass on the validity of a
local ordinance and that, therefore, the Supreme Court had
no jurisdiction to review its decision on the merits. An appeal
from the lower court would have to go first to the Court of
Appeals. Justices Brennan, White, and Marshall dissented on
the ground that the ordinance was palpably bad because of its
vagueness.

Later statutory court decisions declaring various state laws on disorderly conduct, obscenity, and vagrancy unconstitutional as too vague met the same fate.

In 1971 the United States Court of Appeals that sits in New York decided that those decisions did not control the case before it which involved an attack by Black Panthers on harassment by the authorities of the city of Mount Vernon. These had claimed that the Panthers could not sell their newspaper on the streets of the city without taking out a license and paying a fee under a local ordinance. The lower federal court had dismissed the case without a trial. This, said the appeals court, was wrong. There had to be a trial to develop the facts of the claimed harassment and determine whether it had been deliberate. In a footnote which discussed the recent Supreme Court decisions, the court stressed the "chilling" effect on vendors of the paper of the police activities complained of.

When state law permits no appeal within its own court system (as where a very small fine is imposed), direct review can be sought from the United States Supreme Court.

It is essential, in any event, that the case have been decided by the state court by rejection of the federal contention and not on the basis of state law or procedure. To avoid doubt on this score the practice has developed in some states of having the highest court in which the case was decided certify to the United States Supreme Court that the federal claim had been considered and denied. Failure to get such a certificate can be fatal.

The Supreme Court does not always accept a statement by the state court that it has denied relief on some state ground. For instance, in one case the state court claimed that it had rejected the federal claim because the challenger to the constitutionality of an ordinance had not complied with a local rule which required separate challenges to each section of the ordinance. The United States Supreme Court rejected that explanation of the state court's action because the objection

to the ordinance had been framed in such comprehensive
terms that reference to each section would have been mean-
ingless.

Occasionally the Supreme Court has found a way to avoid
injustice even when the state decision has properly rested on
a requirement of state law. In the second Scottsboro appeal
the issue of discrimination against Negroes in the selection of
juries (see section 9b) had been raised at the second trial of
one of the nine defendants, Haywood Patterson. A few days
after Patterson's conviction the same evidence was, by agreement, read into the record at the trial of another of the nine,
Clarence Norris. The convictions of both were appealed to the
Alabama Supreme Court. In Alabama the law requires that
the testimony taken at the trial in question-and-answer form
be changed into what is called narrative form. The record so
prepared then has to be certified by the judge who tried the
case; it is known as the bill of exceptions. These records were
prepared by lawyers in New York who had worked for the defense. On account of an airplane's delay the Patterson record
did not arrive in time for it to be certified within the period
fixed by law; the Norris record arrived in time. The state
court, therefore, considered and rejected the claim of discrimination in Norris' case, but refused to consider it in Patterson's. The Supreme Court granted certiorari in both cases, reversed the Norris conviction on the merits (see section 9b) and
sent the Patterson case back to the Alabama Supreme Court.
It noted that the crucial testimony had been taken in the Patterson case and asked the Alabama court to reconsider its ruling in the light of the United States Supreme Court finding
that there had been discrimination in the selection of the
juries. To the credit of the Alabama court it did reconsider
and set Patterson's conviction aside. (Later Patterson was
convicted after a third trial. This time the Supreme Court refused to review the case, but ultimately Patterson was released.)

When a state conviction has been challenged on federal

constitutional grounds all the way through the state judicial system, so that state remedies have been "exhausted," recourse can be had to the federal courts in habeas corpus proceedings (see section 21e). When a conviction has been carried on appeal through the state courts it is not necessary to try other kinds of possible state relief before going into the federal court for habeas corpus.

The rule of "exhaustion" has not always been strictly adhered to by the Supreme Court. It was relaxed in a very unusual situation. Three men were convicted of killings on confessions procured from all three under the same circumstances. Two of them carried their contention that the confessions had been improperly obtained through the state courts and, when they lost there, instituted habeas corpus proceedings in a federal court. After their federal appeal proved successful the third man, who had not appealed in the state court, also went to a federal court. The United States Supreme Court upheld his right to do so under these extraordinary circumstances. It noted that he had feared to appeal to the state court because of the possibility that if that court granted a new trial he might have been sentenced to death.

Whenever a habeas corpus proceeding is properly brought in a federal court that court must take testimony with regard to the claim asserted unless it finds that the facts had been fully developed in the state court. When the state has not provided a hearing the federal courts can either require it to do so or hold the hearing itself.

If the federal court rejects the contentions raised in the habeas corpus proceeding an appeal to the United States Court of Appeals is possible only if the judge of the lower court grants a certificate of "probable cause"—that is, that the issue is important enough to warrant an appeal. If he refuses, an application for such certificate can be made to a judge of the Court of Appeals, or as a last resort, to one of the Justices of the Supreme Court. The Court of Appeals, by a panel of three judges, can issue such certificate.

Extradition proceedings, such as those in New York against Angela Davis, highlight an old problem in this field. Attempts have often been made to prevent extradition from one state to another on the ground that some constitutional right would be lost because of peculiarities in the demanding state's judicial procedures or biases. These attempts have always been denied, as was Miss Davis', on the ground that a federal court may not intervene in advance of actual infringement of rights. Miss Davis will, therefore, have to raise any constitutional issues she may have in the courts of California in the first place, with the right to go into federal court if unsuccessful there.

50. Federal Infringements

When the federal government has started a law suit or an administrative proceeding the person affected has no technical obstacles to raising any constitutional issue he believes is involved. But it is essential that the claim of constitutional violation be raised at the earliest possible moment and consistently brought up on all occasions.

A person convicted in a federal court used to be able to raise constitutional issues by way of habeas corpus. Now the law requires him to make a motion in the court which sentenced him under a provision of the federal law known as 28 U.S.C. 2255. This can be done even when an appeal from the conviction has been unsuccessful.

A federal prisoner who is indigent and wants to appeal *in forma pauperis* is entitled to a transcript and a lawyer to help him persuade the appellate court that his appeal has such merit as to give him the right to appeal in that manner.

A special situation exists in deportation proceedings. There the alien, if in custody, can bring habeas corpus proceedings in the federal courts and in any case can bring an action for a declaratory judgment (see section 14B).

On the other hand, if an individual wants to take the initiative, as by suit to challenge the constitutionality of a federal statute or of its application, he must be able to show that more than $10,000 is involved, except where a particular law permits otherwise, as, for instance, in the District of Columbia. The same is true when the suit is against some federal official. Otherwise suit must be brought in the state courts.

When the suit is against a federal official it can be brought in a federal court, even where the "jurisdictional" amount is involved, only if the official is charged with violating a duty imposed by the Constitution or an Act of Congress or when the plaintiff and the official sued are citizens of different states.

While various Civil Rights Acts permit suit for their violation regardless of the amount involved, these are directed mainly against state infringements. However, if it can be shown that a federal official acted with state officials or private persons under color of state law then suit can be brought in a federal court.

51. Who Can Raise a Constitutional Issue

The United States Supreme Court will not decide a constitutional issue, even if it had been passed on by the state court or lower federal court, unless it concludes that the person who raised the issue had a "justiciable" interest, that is, that he was really affected by the acts or law he complained of. This has been called "standing."

Generally a person whose only interest is that of a taxpayer has no standing. But in 1968 the Court ruled that where a First Amendment right was involved a taxpayer might sue.

Suit was started in a federal court in New York by payers of
federal income tax to prevent the use of federal funds to
finance instruction in religious schools and purchase textbooks for use in such schools. The lower court had ruled, on
the basis of an old Supreme Court decision, that the plaintiffs
had no standing. The Supreme Court distinguished the old
case from the new one, reversed the dismissal of the latter,
and sent the case back to the lower court for consideration of
the merits. Chief Justice Warren said (392 U.S. 83):

> The taxpayer-appellants in this case have satisfied both nex-
> uses to support their claim of standing under the test we an-
> nounce today. Their constitutional challenge is made to an exer-
> cise by Congress of its power under Art. I, § 8, to spend for the
> general welfare, and the challenged program involves a sub-
> stantial expenditure of federal tax funds. In addition, appel-
> lants have alleged that the challenged expenditures violate the
> Establishment and Free Exercise Clauses of the First Amend-
> ment. Our history vividly illustrates that one of the specific evils
> feared by those who drafted the Establishment Clause and
> fought for its adoption was that the taxing and spending power
> would be used to favor one religion over another or to support
> religion in general. James Madison, who is generally recognized
> as the leading architect of the religion clauses of the First
> Amendment, observed in his famous Memorial and Remon-
> strance Against Religious Assessments that "the same author-
> ity which can force a citizen to contribute three pence only of
> his property for the support of any one establishment, may
> force him to conform to any other establishment in all cases
> whatsoever." The concern of Madison and his supporters was
> quite clearly that religious liberty ultimately would be the vic-
> tim if government could employ its taxing and spending powers
> to aid one religion over another or to aid religion in general. The
> Establishment Clause was designed as a specific bulwark
> against such potential abuses of governmental power, and that
> clause of the First Amendment operates as a specific constitu-
> tional limitation upon the exercise by Congress of the taxing
> and spending power conferred by Art. I, § 8.

The Court has held that organizations have sufficient standing to protect the rights of their members, as when several organizations were threatened with being listed as subversive by the Attorney General. So the NAACP was allowed to challenge a state law which required disclosure of the names of its members in that state (see section 2). Similarly book publishers had the right to challenge action taken by a Rhode Island commission in connection with allegedly obscene material, though the action was directed at booksellers, not publishers. So a member of a labor union was given the right to challenge a Louisiana law that created a commission to look into possible labor crime.

On the other hand, the first case taken to the Supreme Court to test Connecticut's birth control law was thrown out by the Supreme Court because it was instituted by persons (two doctors and two women) who had not actually been threatened with prosecution. The majority noted that there had, in fact, been no prosecutions under the law. Years later when a prosecution was instituted the Court decided that the law invaded the privacy of the married state (see section 2).

In 1969 the Court rejected an attack on the constitutionality of a New York law that banned the distribution of anonymous election material on the ground that the man who had brought the suit had become a judge and was not likely to run again for office.

In 1971 the Court unanimously ruled that persons not actually threatened with state criminal prosecution had no right to institute a suit in federal court to challenge a state law they believed unconstitutional. The following year the Court rejected a challenge to surveillance by the Army where the plaintiffs could show no harm to themselves.

52. Mootness

The Supreme Court will not consider any question if circumstances have so changed that the issue has become academic,

or moot. But in certain circumstances the doctrine of mootness is ignored. If a person in custody applies to the Court for
a writ of habeas corpus his case does not become academic if
he is freed before the proceeding has run its course, and the
convicted person had, during the long time the case was in
the courts, finished serving his sentence. On the other hand a
criminal case does not become moot, even with the death of
the defendant, if liability for costs is involved. Release on
parole will not moot a habeas corpus proceeding if the
conditions of parole are onerous by restricting freedom of
movement and choice of occupation, or where the conviction
may carry serious consequences.

Mootness resulted in the dismissal of two obscenity misdemeanor cases from New York because the cases reached the
Supreme Court more than a year after suspended sentences
had been given, that being the period in which the defendants
might have been sent to jail. Later the Court modified the
harshness of these decisions. In one case it was because the
conviction, despite the suspended sentence, might result in
loss of the renewal of a lunchcounter license; in another because, under state law, the earlier conviction could be used as
an attack on the defendant's credibility if he should later be
convicted of some crime. The Court has not been willing to
consider the impact of misdemeanor convictions as possible
bars to employment or professional careers.

An interesting variant of the mootness doctrine occurred in
a case involving the "White Supremacist" National States
Rights party. On the ground that this organization was making insulting and threatening remarks against Negroes and
Jews, the authorities obtained an injunction that was good
for only ten days. Despite the fact that the ten days had long
since elapsed, the Supreme Court heard the case on the merits
because the state court's opinion continued to play a substantial role in restricting the organization's activities.

53. New Decisions

As the Supreme Court from time to time has handed down decisions expanding the areas of protected liberties, attempts have been made to apply the new doctrines to old cases. These have been successful only to a limited extent.

The Supreme Court has applied its new rules retroactively to criminal cases where the fairness of the trial might have been affected. Generally the problem has arisen when a habeas corpus proceeding is instituted by a prisoner in the hope that he can have the new ruling brought to bear on his old case and so get a new trial at which he may be able to vindicate himself. The Court has allowed this in a number of situations involving such questions as the right to counsel, the prohibition against the use of a codefendant's statement or the use of a witness's statement given at a preliminary hearing, the rule that a plea of guilty cannot be accepted in the absence of counsel, the right of an indigent to a free transcript of the trial proceedings for the purpose of appeal.

In 1971 the Court, by a 5-4 decision, gave retroactive effect to the earlier ruling that a gambling tax law was unconstitutional where an attempt was made to forfeit property. Chief Justice Burger and Justices White, Stewart, and Blackmun dissented. But in another case decided at the same time Justice Harlan joined those dissenters to sustain a conviction for income tax evasion where the evidence had been obtained from returns filed under the gambling tax law.

Retroactive effect has also not been given to decisions which required police to warn suspects before taking statements and which barred comment by a prosecutor that a defendant had not taken the stand.

The Court has not given its new decisions retroactive application in situations involving various questions: the barring in state courts of evidence obtained as the result of an illegal search, wiretap, or electronic eavesdropping; restrictions on

the use of lineup identifications; the requirement of jury
trials in state courts; the ruling that defendants have a right
to counsel even at preliminary hearings; and the ruling that a
soldier cannot be tried by court-martial for an offense that is
not service-connected.

54. Some Trends

The fears of civil libertarians that the four Justices
appointed by President Nixon would transform the Supreme
Court into a bastion of conservative legal thought have been
only partially realized. In the last few years there have been a
large number of 4-3 and 5-4 decisions considered unfavorable
by civil libertarians. In most of the 5-4 cases Justice White
sided with the four Nixon appointees. But there were some
pro-civil liberties 5-4 decisions in which Justice White joined
Justices Douglas, Brennan, Marshall, and Stewart and all
four Nixon appointees were in dissent. There have been a
number of close decisions in which the Nixon appointees were
divided. As yet there has been no case that expressly
overruled any of the Warren Court's determinations, which
greatly expanded the areas of protected liberty.

Appendixes

Appendix 1: The Bill of Rights

ARTICLE [I]

Congress shall make no law respecting an establishment of religion, or prohibiting the free exercise thereof; or abridging the freedom of speech, or of the press; or the right of the people peaceably to assemble, and to petition the Government for a redress of grievances.

ARTICLE [II]

A well regulated Militia, being necessary to the security of a free State, the right of the people to keep and bear Arms, shall not be infringed.

ARTICLE [III]

No Soldier shall, in time of peace be quartered in any house, without the consent of the Owner, nor in time of war, but in a manner to be prescribed by law.

ARTICLE [IV]

The right of the people to be secure in their persons, houses, papers, and effects, against unreasonable searches and seizures, shall not be violated, and no Warrants shall issue, but upon probable cause, supported by Oath or affirmation, and particularly describing the place to be searched, and the persons or things to be seized.

ARTICLE [V]

No person shall be held to answer for a capital, or otherwise infamous crime, unless on a presentment or indictment of a Grand Jury, except in cases arising in the land or naval forces, or in the Militia, when in actual service in time of War or public danger; nor shall any person be subject for the same offence to be twice put in jeopardy of life or limb; nor shall be compelled in any criminal case to be a witness against himself, nor be deprived of life, liberty, or property, without due process of law; nor shall private property be taken for public use, without just compensation.

ARTICLE [VI]

In all criminal prosecutions, the accused shall enjoy the right to a speedy and public trial, by an impartial jury of the State and district wherein the crime shall have been committed, which district shall have been previously ascertained by law, and to be informed of the nature and cause of the accusation; to be confronted with the witnesses against him; to have compulsory process for obtaining Witnesses in his favor, and to have the Assistance of Counsel for his defence.

ARTICLE [VII]

In Suits at common law, where the value in controversy shall exceed twenty dollars, the right of trial by jury shall be preserved, and no fact tried by a jury, shall be otherwise reexamined in any Court of the United States, than according to the rules of the common law.

ARTICLE [VIII]

Excessive bail shall not be required, nor excessive fines imposed, nor cruel and unusual punishments inflicted.

ARTICLE [IX]

The enumeration in the Constitution, of certain rights, shall not be construed to deny or disparage others retained by the people.

ARTICLE [X]

The powers not delegated to the United States by the Constitution, nor prohibited by it to the States, are reserved to the States respectively, or to the people.

Appendix 2: The Post-Civil War Amendments

ARTICLE [XIII]

Section 1. Neither slavery nor involuntary servitude, except as a punishment for crime whereof the party shall have been duly convicted, shall exist within the United States, or any place subject to their jurisdiction.

Section 2. Congress shall have power to enforce this article by appropriate legislation.

ARTICLE [XIV]

Section 1. All persons born or naturalized in the United States, and subject to the jurisdiction thereof, are citizens of the United States and of the State wherein they reside. No State shall make or enforce any law which shall abridge the privileges or immunities of citizens of the United States; nor shall any State deprive any person of life, liberty, or property, without due process of law; nor deny to any person within its jurisdiction the equal protection of the laws.

Section 2. Representatives shall be apportioned among the several States according to their respective numbers, counting the whole number of persons in each State, excluding Indians not taxed. But when the right to vote at any election for the choice of electors for President and Vice President of the United States, Representatives in Congress, the Executive and

Judicial officers of a State, or the members of the Legislature thereof, is denied to any of the male inhabitants of such State, being twenty-one years of age, and citizens of the United States, or in any way abridged, except for participation in rebellion, or other crime, the basis of representation therein shall be reduced in the proportion which the number of such male citizens shall bear to the whole number of male citizens twenty-one years of age in such State.

Sections 3 and 4 are omitted as they dealt only with temporary matters growing out of the Civil War.

Section 5. The Congress shall have power to enforce, by appropriate legislation, the provisions of this article.

ARTICLE [XV]

Section 1. The right of citizens of the United States to vote shall not be denied or abridged by the United States or by any State on account of race, color, or previous condition of servitude.

Section 2. The Congress shall have power to enforce this article by appropriate legislation.

Appendix 3: Justices of the Supreme Court, 1945-1973

(a—year appointed; d—year of death; r—year of retirement; *—still sitting.)

Harlan F. Stone, Chief Justice (a 1925; as Chief 1941; d 1946)
Owen J. Roberts (a 1930, r 1945)
Hugo L. Black (a 1937, r 1971)
Stanley Reed (a 1938, r 1957)
Felix Frankfurter (a 1939, r 1962)
William O. Douglas* (a 1939)
Frank Murphy (a 1940, d 1949)
Robert H. Jackson (a 1941, d 1954)

Justices of the Supreme Court, 1945-1971

Wiley Rutledge (a 1943, d 1949)
Harold H. Burton (a 1945, r 1958)
Fred Vinson, Chief Justice (a 1946, d 1953)
Tom C. Clark (a 1949, r 1967)
Sherman Minton (a 1949, r 1956)
Earl Warren, Chief Justice (a 1953, r 1969)
John M. Harlan (a 1955, r 1971)
William J. Brennan, Jr.* (a 1956)
Charles E. Whittaker (a 1957, r 1962)
Potter Stewart* (a 1958)
Byron White* (a 1962)
Arthur J. Goldberg (a 1962, r 1965)
Abe Fortas (a 1965, r 1969)
Thurgood Marshall* (a 1967)
*Warren Earl Burger, Chief Justice** (a 1969)
Harry A. Blackmun* (a 1970)
Lewis F. Powell* (a 1972)
William H. Rehnquist* (a 1972)

Index

236

Index

241

Index